Speak first.
Repeat often.

Don't worry too much about the truth.

PJ Lehrer

ISBN 978-0-9897422-4-5

Acknowledgements

A special thanks to Tim Baynes for creating original artwork for the cover of this book. @timbaynes

And another thanks to Doug Ritter for his proofing/input.

But mostly I want to thank my husband Edward Lindquist, not just for his proofing skills, but also his love. You've shown me how sweet this life can be.

Preface

The title of this book is a summary of three key pieces of communications research. The Primacy Effect tells us that we tend to believe the first thing that we hear about a subject. The Ebbinghaus Forgetting Curve shows that a minimum of three exposures are necessary for people to remember a message. And the Illusionary Truth Effect establishes that we mistake familiarity for truth, so that after three exposures we begin to think something is true whether or not it actually is.

In 2017, Richard Thaler won a Nobel Prize in economics for his research about predictable irrationality in decision-making. But isn't that an oxymoron? If something is predictable isn't it by definition rational? It only appears to be irrational to the researchers because they didn't understand or agree with the criteria being used for making the decision. But it's not up to them to decide. We choose. And, personality type, social status and even anthropological factors influence our decision-making.

This book is a curated selection of the research currently available about human behavior that influences our choices. It connects the dots between research theory and current practices to explore the way in which this knowledge is used to create persuasive communications.

The information is arranged in four sections -

1. Whom you talk to (target)
2. What you say (message)
3. How you say it (delivery)
4. Where you say it (media)

Endnotes are included for access to original research sources for additional data. And a glossary has been added for clarity.

Prof. Lehrer

Table of Contents

Part 1
Whom you talk to (target)

Chapter 1. Research

All research is biased. Consider carefully what you use and how you use it.

These days we have more data available than we can handle, so the issue is not the absence of information but rather, the overabundance of it and the need to analyze it properly in order for it to be useful.

The way that we think and feel is influenced by our genetics and environment. Therefore, we are all biased. So it's not a surprise that our research is too. But that doesn't mean that we can't use it to inform our decisions. It does mean that we need to look closely at the data before we do.

Consider the source.

Primary research is developed, fielded and analyzed by the company that commissions it. That makes it the most reliable data available. But it is also very expensive. So, most of us will rely on secondary data - i.e. data that someone else gathers, for our analyses.

The most important factor in the reliability of secondary research is source. Research companies, like Pew Research and Mintel, that make their living selling their data care about its reliability, so they gather it appropriately.

Unfortunately, much of what passes for research on the internet these days is in fact propaganda. So the first question you should ask yourself is - who put out this research and what agenda do they have?

Perhaps the most infamous example of underwriting misleading research was the fake news spread by the tobacco companies beginning in the 1950's. Sadly, their goal was to get people to question the truth behind the compelling anti-smoking health research that was being released at the time by suggesting that it was inaccurate or open to discussion. They were so successful that the total number of cigarettes sold in 1961 was 488 billion, up 32% from 369 billion in 1954.[1]

Therefore, as part of the Tobacco Master Settlement Agreement in 1998, cigarette companies were forced to restrict their advertising, sponsorship, lobbying, and litigation activities, particularly as those activities were seen as targeting youth; and to disband the "Tobacco Institute", "The Center for Indoor Air Research", and "The Council for Tobacco Research," to stop the flow of misleading information.[2]

But the misleading data they shared is still out there. And their tactic of fighting facts with disinformation has been widely adapted by others.

Of course most of the misleading data on the internet is not quite as egregious. The data just promotes the brand being sold by slicing and dicing the data in a way that is to its advantage. Therefore it is always wise to look particularly closely for conflicts of interest in any company sponsored research.

That having been said, unconscious bias is also an issue. A female economist did a study that unearthed the finding that female researchers who co-publish with men, get zero credit for their efforts, even if they are the lead authors. Needless to say, she was planning on writing her future research papers alone.[3]

A subsequent study showed that male researchers used more positive terms in their papers than did female researchers. Yes, they brag - whether warranted or not. But it works. Positive presentation is associated with 9.4% more citations. And citations turn into promotions and grants down the road. The advice of the authors for women - learn to brag.[4]

Unconscious bias permeates everything we do, even algorithms. In the early days of computers, the saying "humans make mistakes, but it takes a computer to really foul things up" was quite popular. It is just as relevant today.

In a study published in "Science" in October 2019, researchers found that an algorithm used widely in health care services has a built-in racial bias. Despite being at similar levels of illness, black patients were classified as lower risk than were white ones. Why? Because the measure being used for "sickness" in the algorithm was health care expenditures. And since society spends less on black patients than white ones, the algorithm understated their true needs.[5] Which brings to mind another saying about computers - "garbage in, garbage out."

Lastly, please note that Google's mobile search is not as robust as it is on desktops/laptops. You will find more and better information on the latter. And since search is influenced by previous behavior, the more legitimate research you seek, the easier it will be to find more like it.

Look at the methodology.

Participant selection is the most important factor in achieving accurate research results. Users and non-users are likely to have different feedback about a brand. And just because you didn't vote in the last election doesn't mean you won't vote in the next one.

The decline in use of land line telephones has created a dilemma for researchers. They can no longer count on telephone surveys to accurately reflect the population at large. Typically, those still using land lines are older, poorer and less educated than average, and therefore, results skew in that direction. Adding data from mobile phones is a must, but then someone has to decide how to weigh the data from the different sources. Add computer surveys to the input and balancing issues become even more complex and subjective.

Failing to weight data properly by adding emphasis to respondents that are underrepresented in the sample can lead to problems projecting results properly. In reviewing the inaccuracy of pre-election polling for the 2016 election, it was noted that most of the polls failed to account for education level, which turned out to be a key factor in predicting choice.[6]

Additional bias results from the participants themselves. All people lie - mostly to protect their self-esteem.[7] That's why 64% of Americans say they are healthy eaters despite the fact that 2/3 of the population is either overweight or obese.[8]

It's also the reason why "vanity sizing" - i.e. deliberately using smaller size labels, works. Smaller size labels evoke more positive self-related mental imagery. As you might expect, the effect is particularly significant among people with low appearance self-esteem.[9]

People are also subject to acquiescence bias, which is the desire to please by providing the correct answer.[10] This is the reason why a question about whether someone has seen a piece of communications can yield a positive response. But deeper probing, like asking for a summary of the data from that communication, can result in playback from a previous older communication from the same company.

How you ask a question matters too. What does being green mean? To Baby Boomers being green means recycling. But to Millennials it means sustainability. Likewise Boomers think eating healthy means avoiding foods high in fat and sugar and watching their weight; while Millennials think it means eating organic and staying hydrated. Therefore it is best to ask specific questions rather than dealing in generalities.

Undoubtedly the type of person who answers a survey is inherently different from those who do not. That's why you should always favor hard data over survey data. The U.S. government is the best source of hard data we have. The sample sizes are huge, the data is based on actions, and it is available in very granular form.

Conversely, be very careful with qualitative research (focus groups), which by definition incorporate very small sample sizes. While you will always learn something by listening to consumers, geographical difference in feedback is so pronounced that typically groups are done in three different locations spread across the country.

Scotts

A campaign under consideration for Scotts Turf Builder involved a couple taking care of their lawn together. In Cincinnati, Ohio the idea was met with disbelief and the resounding statement: "Lawns are men's work. Women belong in the kitchen." When the same creative was shared in a suburb of Philadelphia, the reaction was: "Well I don't know anything about lawns, so if she wants to help out, good for her."

Stimuli is important.

The materials you use for testing will affect outcomes. More finished versions of video storyboards will test better in all testing formats including online. Positioning statements will yield more accurate feedback about strategies because they don't include executional elements. And asking open-ended questions can provoke different responses than a multiple choice question will.

Specifics matter. When asked in 2002 which is more important - domestic policy or foreign policy, 52% chose domestic policy while only 34% said foreign policy. But when asked to choose between domestic policy and "the war on terrorism," only 33% chose domestic policy while 52% chose the war on terrorism.[11]

Ask awkward questions using ranges. Most people are uncomfortable if you ask them their age. Instead offer some age ranges, e.g. 18-24 and 25-39 and ask which group they fall into. Do the same with household income.

It is worth noting that often respondents will tell you that they would be willing to consider something, but they don't think other people will. In a 2019 Ipsos/Daily Beast poll, when Democrats and Independents were asked if they would be comfortable with a female president, 74% said they would, but they believed that only 33% of their neighbors would agree. Which is why both questions need to be asked.[12]

Finally remember that we are hard wired to notice and agree with research that reinforces our beliefs and ignore research that does not. This interpretation bias is yet another way we can be mislead by data.

Sample size matters.

Anecdotal data supplied by your best friend may be interesting, but it is not statistically significant, and therefore not projectable.

When sample sizes are smaller, the margin of error increases. It is not uncommon these days to see polls with a margin of error of +/- 5%, often a differential that is greater than the numbers shown, meaning that statistically speaking the options are tied.[13] And yet, despite this fact, the results are discussed as if they are meaningful when they actually aren't.

Bigger data bases are better because they make it easier to identify majority trends. AncestryDNA has 15 million users, 23andMe has 10 million. More than 300 million people use Chrome. With databases of that size, projections become more accurate.

The devil is in the details

Research reflecting broad trends is often at odds with data based on smaller segments.

Consider educational attainment. As of 2018, 33% of Americans 18+ have a B.A. degree or higher. For New York State it's the same. For NYC it goes up to 39%. But for the 10021 zip code on the Upper East Side of Manhattan it's a whopping 81%, reflecting a high presence of managers, educators and doctors who live and work in the area.

Educational Attainment: 2018 (5 - year estimates)

	Total U.S.	NY State	NYC	10021
B.A. Degree	20.1%	18.6%	22.8%	38.9%
Graduate/ Professional Degree	12.6%	14.1%	16.1%	41.8%
Total	32.6%	32.6%	38.6%	80.7%

data.census.gov/cedsci/advanced

Other research is similarly affected. When it comes to matters of health, ethnicity seems to play a key role. African-Americans have higher amounts of vitamin D deficiency because darker skin does not absorb the UV rays necessary to create it as well as lighter skin does.

A 2018 study about whether vitamin D supplements had any health benefits, reached the general conclusion that they did not. With one exception. Vitamin D supplementation in African-Americans reduced cancer risk by 23%. Why? Evidence suggests that low vitamin D levels negatively affect the immune system.[14]

Check the expiration date.

Research doesn't have to be new to be usable. Ebbinghaus developed his Forgetting Curve in 1885. And he developed it using a sample size of one - himself! But his work was so seminal that other researchers began building on it immediately with sequential research that also served to validate the original findings.

On the other hand, research about consumer trends and media use must be recent to be accurate because of the fluid nature of both.

As the different generations experience life cycle milestones like marriage and children, their beliefs and brand usage change significantly. And new media comes and goes these days. In general, research data can be considered accurate until it is contradicted by newer studies on the subject, as long as milestones are kept in mind.

That having been said we are definitely in the age of BC/AC - i.e. before Covid-19 and after Covid-19. This once in a century global pandemic will have far reaching consequences that cannot even be imagined at this early stage of the event.

Already, we are seeing significant changes in consumer behavior due the pandemic and its consequences - toilet paper sales were up 65% in March/April, lottery ticket sales were down, and Netflix added 16 million new subscribers in 1Q 2020.

There is no way to tell at this time how many of these changes will become permanent. But at the very least, any research that was done BC (before Covid-19) should be reviewed very carefully prior to use.

Chapter 2. Targets

At a minimum, target descriptions should include gender, age range and a plus one.

All communications should begin with an analysis of the intended audience. Who are they? How can we describe them? What do they do? Where do they live? What's important to them? The more detail you can provide, the better able you will be to connect with your audience.

Consider this description of the typical Adele fan...

- 62% female
- 25-44 (28% 50+)
- children
- drinks light beer & Aquafina water
- 20% more likely to smell personal-care products before buying
- 81% more likely to read *Parents* magazine
- 60% more likely to work as technicians or other support staff in the health-care industry
- 69% more likely to play soccer
- They still buy albums

Data source: Nielsen[1]

Heavy Users/Primary Target

Research has demonstrated the applicability of Joseph Juran's 80/20 rule, also known as the Pareto Principle, to just about everything. When applied to marketing the principle says that in any given category, 80 percent of a product is bought by 20 percent of its consumers.[2] The pattern is pervasive, even extending into unexpected areas - like Covid-19, where 20% of the people are responsible for 80% of the spread.[3]

In marketing, we call these individuals heavy users.

Most companies will begin by identifying these heavy users and designating them as the primary target. This makes perfect sense. A company's first priority should always be to maintain current customers, because retaining customers costs less than finding new ones. It is also easier to convince current customers to use a company's product or service more frequently, than it is to get a new customer. And finally, when a company does want to find new users, they are most likely to be similar in profile to current users.

It is important to note that heavy users and light users have different priorities and therefore need to be approached with different strategies. For instance, a heavy user of swimsuits might respond to the following three rationale points - 1. long lasting 2. fits well 3. good sale prices. Note that what isn't included in that proposition - looks good - is likely to be the number one selling point for a light user.

A classic example of a marketer making this mistake was the infamous "Got Milk" campaign. While the effort ran for decades and had lots of fans, milk sales continued to decline throughout its duration. A closer look as to why, unearths the fact that the strategy - people feel deprived when they run out of milk - was only relevant to heavy users as lighter users rarely ran out of milk, or cared much when they did.[4]

Secondary Users/Niche Target

Thanks to the fragmentation of media and the growth of the Internet it is now possible to reach niche targets (i.e. smaller, more well-defined segments) effectively. Therefore most marketers now target numerous user segments in their marketing plans.

One example is hemorrhoid products. The primary target for them is Men, ages 45-60, who are overweight. But since 20-50 percent of pregnant women get hemorrhoids, it makes sense to run a smaller budget secondary campaign targeting Women 18-45, who are pregnant. Since these women can be reached very efficiently by a variety of targeted media, with low out-of-pocket costs, it is worth investing money in them, even if they will only use the product for a limited time.[5]

Sometimes new information is discovered about a product/service that would make it appealing to a niche target. For instance, a significant amount of research has been published about the health benefits of lycopene, which can be found in tomatoes. Currently, V8 targets Women 18-49 with children under 12, using a broad health story. But what if V8 did a limited campaign targeting Men 50-65 in poor health with the message: "Drink V8 and live longer?" Would it add incremental sales?[6]

Meal delivery services, which were struggling prior to Covid-19, are partnering with populations that have special dietary needs. Blue Apron is now working with Weight Watchers, offering "WW Approved" recipes.[7] And Mt. Sinai has taken an equity stake in Epicured which offers low-FODMAP and gluten-free meals to patients.[8]

Neither of these efforts is designed to replace marketing to primary targets, but it is likely that they are adding to the companies' bottom line as both programs are continuing in 2020.

Ultimately, what will emerge from this approach to selecting target markets is a variety of target segments that will require entirely different communication plans and messaging. What makes this approach both possible and utterly necessary is the continued fragmentation of media, culture and tribal allegiances and the presence of various personality types in the population.

At the end of the day, the more narrowly you define your audience the easier it will be to connect with them.

Gender

Start by defining your target's gender. While it may be tempting to say "adults" since clearly everyone could buy your brand, the reality is that they are not.

Remember you are only trying to appeal to the heaviest users - the 20% who do 80% of the consumption. And most, if not all brands, skew either male or female.

Even if a particular product did appeal equally to males and females you would still want to select one gender or the other for your communication efforts because men and women do not think, feel or act the same way. They consume different media. They even use different vocabularies - women "diet," men "get in shape."

Northwestern Mutual

When Northwestern Mutual decided to focus on females in a 2018 campaign, they first repositioned the company as a financial planning company rather than an insurance company. Then they developed their first television commercial with a storyline focused solely on a woman and her career, which they ran on lifestyle programming such as Bravo and Food Network. They also created online content (how-to articles) about preparing for maternity leave, networking groups for women, improving hiring prospects, and boosting earning power.

The results were impressive. Within the first week of the campaign they saw triple-digit growth for key performance indicators (KPIs) including traffic, leads and brand mentions online. Ultimately they realized a...

66% increase in unique visits to website
30% increase in social brand mentions
400%+ increase in leads
18% increase in social followers[9]

All because they recognized that men and women are different and need to be approached differently by marketers.

Age Range

It is important when identifying a target to give a specific age range because vague terms such as "middle-age" are subject to interpretation bias. And, the older you are, the older "old" gets.

Opened ended targets, e.g. 65+ are problematic as well. People 65 - 75 are very different from people 76 - 85. Ditto 18 and under, which includes babies, children and teens.

It is important to take note of which generation the target belongs to because different generations have been impacted by different life events. Someone once said to me "I find that people who remember President Kennedy's death are very different from those who do not." He was recognizing the difference between Baby Boomers and Gen X. Similarly, Millennials remember 9/11 and Gen Z does not.

Not surprisingly then, the generations think and feel differently. They have different communication preferences, consume different media, and even look for different features in a hotel. So if the next time you stay at a Marriott you find a smaller closet, no desk, and more outlets, you can thank the Millennials.[10]

Different generations even have a different sense of humor.

A classic research study from 2001 determined that the most successful form of humor for persuasion was irony.[11] But an effort to replicate the results of the study in 2016 failed. Why? Because the stimuli used in the initial research was a "Far Side" cartoon. So Baby Boomers got it, while

Millennials did not. It begs the question of whether the results from the original research could be replicated if the stimuli were updated.[12]

Note that there is no absolute authority defining the generations, or even naming them. But most people defer to Pew Research on the matter in order to better use the data that they publish.

Here are the relevant dates and population size as of 2020, based on Pew Research definitions and 2018 census data updates...

Silent Generation:	23MM	b 1928-1945; ages 75 - 92
Baby Boomers:	72MM	b 1946-1964; ages 56 - 74
Gen X:	65MM	b 1965-1980; ages 40 - 55
Millennials (Y):	72MM	b 1981-1996; ages 24 - 39
Gen Z:	65MM	b 1997-2012; ages 8 - 23

Source: Pew Research, census.gov[13]

Pew shifted the age range for Millennials slightly in 2019 in recognition of the fact that 9/11 was a defining moment for the generation. They believe that everyone who was over the age of five at the time remembers the event well enough to be influenced by it. So they adjusted accordingly.

It seems likely based on current events, that the age range for Gen Z will be similarly adjusted to account for the influence of the Covid-19 pandemic.

When you select a target you are looking for a coherent group that shares similar characteristics.

You shouldn't include an entire generation because you also need to take into consideration the fact that people are going through different lifecycle stages. Older Baby Boomers may be retired, while younger ones are still working. Older Millennials are likely to be married with children, while younger ones may still be single. Be particularly careful when looking at data for Gen Z as the younger end of the group is currently 8. Why would they be interested in politics at that age?

The chart on the previous page notes the size of the generations. It is easy to see why attention has shifted from Baby Boomers to Millennials in the U.S., where they are the largest generation. Globally Gen Z is the largest generation. As of 2020, the average age of Americans is 45. The median age (as many people below the number as above) is 38. And the mode (most people) is 30.

Plus One

The "plus one" is a differentiator, i.e. a descriptor that sets the target apart from others. The goal is to find a plus one that captures the essence of your target so that it provides direction for strategic development.

If you ran a health club, based on the research cited below, you could define your target as: Women (gender) 25-34 (age range) who are single (plus one).

- Gender: 92% of 13-33-year-old females say it's cool to work out these days.[14]
- Age Range: 33% of Millennials belong to gyms - the highest percentage of the generations.[15]
- Plus One: Today only 30% of young adults are married down from 59% in 1978.[16]

While the inclusion of that plus one does help us to understand the target better, something more specific would be more useful.

What if instead, you defined your target as: Women (gender) 25-34 (age range) who want to meet someone (plus one).

- Plus One: 50% of gym-goers claim they go just to check out the opposite sex.[17]

This differentiator provides infinitely more insight into the target's mindset.

If your brand is a cosmetic then you might go with this: Women (gender) 25-34 (age range) who think a new look might help them get more dates (plus one).

Other examples...

- Men 45-60 who enjoy mountain biking.

- Dads 24-39 with kids under 18 who are cooking more so their families will be healthier.
- Women 23-33 who care about the environment because they enjoy outdoor sports.
- Men 18-24 who want to eat healthier.

You can begin to see how capturing consumer mindset right from the beginning of the process will create better results.

Differentiators

As mentioned in the beginning of the chapter, the more you know about your target the better.
So in addition to gender, age range and a plus one, you can consider the following when generating a target profile.
Focus on just those characteristics that separate the target from everyone else - the differentiators.

Typically we start by considering demographics, defined as: "Population or consumer statistics regarding socioeconomic factors such as age, income, sex, occupation, education, family size and the like."[18]

Below are some additional demographic areas you might want to consider when defining your target market. Please note that this list is meant to be a thought starter, rather than comprehensive.

Marital status
Household income (range)
Children (age range)

Education
Employment (full/part time; trade, professional, healthcare workers, teachers, etc.)
Ethnicity/Heritage (more specific is better but some data may only be available for broader categories i.e., Hispanics, African-Americans, White, Asian-Americans)
Geography (Global, National, Regional, Local, Top cities)

Next consider psychographics. These are "Criteria for segmenting consumers by lifestyle, attitudes, beliefs, values, personality, buying motives, and/or extent of product usage."[19]

Examples of psychographics include:

Pets
Food
Hobbies
Sports
Religion
Culture
Personality traits
Product usage
Media consumption

Going back to the description of Adele's target at the beginning of the chapter, you can see that it includes some differentiators from each of these lists. You would be wise to do the same.

Chapter 3. Tribes

Whom we affiliate with influences our thoughts and behavior.

A study published in *The American Journal of Health*, found that if your friends are overweight, so are you. That's because we change our habits to mirror those of our friends, even if we are unaware that we are doing it.

Remember the last time you went to dinner with friends? Did someone order a drink? If they did, did everyone else? What about dessert?[1]

We all belong to a variety of tribes that influence our behavior. The closer the association we have with the tribe, the more likely we are to follow their cues.

They can be based on racial, religious, geographical or social preferences, also passions. The Internet is accelerating the formation of tribes as it removes geographic limitations, allowing like minded individuals to connect no matter where they live.

What we are most interested in is the commonalities between group members that separate them from the population at large and bind them together with each other. We can use those to establish stronger connections with the target.

For instance, the tribe that I affiliate with most is New Yorkers. Do you want to know the quickest way to annoy a New Yorker? Walk slowly on the sidewalk. How do I know that I am not the only one who feels this way? Because one day someone drew a chalk line down the sidewalk on 5th Avenue and wrote "tourists" on one side and "locals" on the other. It made me smile.

So did this ad from Manhattan Mini Storage who definitely understands their target.

"In My Father's House There Are Many Rooms." -- John 14:2

Clearly , Jesus Was Not A New Yorker.

Storage starting at $29[2]

Other people may not get us, but we get each other. As my niece Jessica, a recent arrival to Manhattan commented -- she understands @overheardnewyork a lot better now. On the other hand, this ad probably wouldn't work outside of NYC even if you changed the location reference. The humor is too closely tied to a New York state of mind.

Thanks to the Internet, tribes today are transcending country borders. In May/June 2020, following the killing of George Floyd, protests against racism and police brutality spread throughout the U.S. They were also held in Britain, Germany, Denmark, Italy, New Zealand, Spain, Canada, Brazil and Japan. While some of the protests overseas may have been about showing solidarity with the U.S., the toppling of a slave trader statue in Bristol, England suggests that the U.S. isn't the only place where racism and police violence resonate.[3]

When thinking about tribes, think broadly. People can connect over a variety of things sometimes in ways that surprise us.

The next time you stay in a hotel room you may see a sign that says "Would you like to reuse your towel and save the environment?" About 35% of the people who see this sign will reuse their towels. But if we up the ante by adding a descriptive norm saying: "Join your fellow guests in reusing your towels," 44% will reuse their towels.

What proved even more powerful though was the use of provincial norms - i.e. norms of one's local setting and circumstances. In this case guests were told that people who had stayed in the same room they were now in had reused their towels. When they read this, the reuse rate rose to 49%. So the need to belong to the tribe prevailed even when the only thing they had in common was staying in the same hotel room temporarily.[4]

In face to face negotiations something as simple as ordering the same meal can create a bond that builds trust and leads to quicker negotiations.[5] So a simple business lunch is not as simple as it seems. And, anyone who has experienced one knows that discussing business on these occasions is considered to be in poor taste. Instead the goal in sharing a meal is to find common ground which will ease future interactions.

Ethnicity

The United States is rapidly turning into a minority-majority country. According to the latest census projections, by 2045, the majority of America will be non-white. The population under 18 already is.[6]

So it makes sense to consider ethnicity when selecting tribes. It is important to note however, that while research refers to "Hispanics," there is no such thing as a Hispanic. There are

Mexicans, Puerto Ricans, Columbians, etc. To truly connect, you will need to drill down to the appropriate sub-culture.

And remember that Asian-Americans, the fastest growing demographic group in the U.S. include Indian-Americans who are currently the best educated and wealthiest minority group in the country. 72% have college degrees and their median household income is $100K, roughly twice as much as average.[7]

In the past few decades research has revealed that North Americans and East Asians have different cognitive styles. North Americans are more likely to use rules and formal logic to categorize objects and understand events; while East Asians are more likely to use intuitive reasoning and relationships to do the same. East Asians are also more likely to consider situational causal factors. In short, Americans are more analytical and Asians are more holistic.[8]

Why? Because Asian societies emphasize the "we" while Americans emphasize the "me." In Asian societies maintaining harmony is important. In America, not so much.

It appears that these cultural differences are not location specific, which means that Asian-Americans (including ABC's, i.e. American Born Chinese) are more contextual than are other Americans. It seems logical to assume that additional research would unearth differences between other ethnic groups as well. That is why it is so important to segment targets into coherent groups before attempting to understand and connect with them.

Pets

People are very passionate about their pets. Consider dog owners. 62% of Americans have at least one pet in the household, 71% of those at least one dog, and 95% of them consider their pets to be part of the family. Americans spend more than $9 billion on dog food annually, and total US spending on pet care in 2019 was $95.7 billion.[9]

What's perhaps even more interesting is the patterns that emerge when we cross reference dog ownership with age. Gen Xers own the most pets, but Millennials are the most likely to buy their pets birthday presents -- 54% do.[10] It's no wonder that dog friendly hotels and restaurants are springing up, and *The New York Daily News* is running edit about doggie cupcakes - a real bargain at $2.50 each.[11]

But you don't need to be selling dog related products or services to tap into people's fondness for their pets. Match.com partnered with PetSmart charities on pet-friendly dating events after a survey showed that 80% of singles are pet lovers.[12]

And apparently Subaru's research showed that their target is so enamored of their dogs that the company went from commercials which merely included dogs to ones that now feature the dogs driving cars.

LGBTQ

Subaru actually divides their target into five distinct segments - educators, health-care professionals, IT people, outdoorsy types and Lesbians.

When reviewing their sales data, Subaru noted that they were extremely popular with single mothers. This led to some additional data mining which unearthed the fact that Lesbians like Subarus. So in 1996, Subaru began actively marketing to them. A radical move at a time when Congress was passing "The Defense of Marriage Act."[13]

These days though, NYC's Gay Pride Parade is overflowing with corporate sponsors. All types of brands are marketing to the tribe. And since so many have been successful, more are jumping on the wagon all the time. In 2018, after three years of declining engagement ring sales, Tiffany decided to reach out to the LGBTQ community and minorities. Sales of engagement rings rose 11%.[14]

Passions

The growth of the Internet and social media has enabled tribes based on passions to flourish as it has removed physical proximity as a requirement for membership. Easily reached online, they are now being courted offline too since we have seen several examples of the effectiveness of this approach.

The Mann Center in Philadelphia holds videogame concerts. The shows attract as many as 6,500 people, roughly double the attendance at classical concerts. Many come in costume. And they spend as much as $13K on souvenirs - action figures, posters, and t-shirts - versus $3K for a typical concert.[15]

Fashionistas have proven to be a good target for both ballets and museums. The Met's *Heavenly Bodies* exhibit attracted 1.6 million viewers, the most ever for an exhibit at the museum. That exhibit appealed to two tribes. The Vatican vestments brought in Catholics/Christians and the fashion interpretations of them brought in Fashionistas.[16]

Meanwhile, retail has turned to Broadway shows to increase its social media profile. Bloomindales teamed with *Dear Evan Hansen* to turn their dressing room into a selfie worthy private lounge complete with a "twitter mirror."[17] Brooks Brothers dressed *Falsetto's* leading men, and Ann Taylor has hosted in-store panel discussions for *Waitress* fans.[18]

Partnerships

Finally, in the past few years we have seen numerous examples of companies working together when they find a common niche target. Hyatt has even selected different partners for different brands. Park Hyatt has partnered with *National Geographic* to attract more photographers, while Hyatt Centric partnered with Sofar Sounds - a company that puts on small pop-up concerts, to attract music lovers.[19]

With the right data and a little imagination, the possibilities are endless.

Chapter 4. Niche Target Recommendation

This is an example of a recommendation for a new niche target.

McCormick Spices Niche Target Recommendation

This provides a recommendation that McCormick Spices implement a niche marketing plan targeting Men 18-24, who want to eat healthier.

Background

McCormick's primary target is Women 25-45 with children under 18. Their website is gender neutral and features many recipes. Their current marketing focuses on the company's 130 years of longevity. Neither their website nor their messaging focuses on the health benefits of spices.

Recommendation/Rationale

We recommend that McCormick Spices implement the "Sprinkle Some McCormick On It" campaign, targeted to Men 18-24 who want to eat healthier.

This recommendation is based on the following rationale:

1. Men 18-24 have financial power

As of 2018, there are 15.7 million Men 18-24 in the U.S. representing 9.7% of the total population. (2018)

It is estimated that globally Gen Z has over $140 billion in buying power. (Davis, 2020) In the U.S., they spent $78 billion in restaurants in 2016. (Valdez, 2018)

And despite what you may have heard, 42% of Men 18-24 do not live with their parents. 29% of them are married. (2017)

2. They want to eat healthier

67% of Gen Z care about the nutritional content of their food. (Valdez, 2018) They are more likely to look for organic or natural foods, and prefer foods without artificial ingredients. They are also more likely to be vegetarians (7%). (Granderson, 2019)

Almost half (41%) say they would pay more for foods they perceive as healthier (2020) And, in the past year, 28% of 18-24 year-olds tried the Paleo diet, 26% went gluten-free, and 24% tried Whole 30. (Sloan, 2019)

Spices and herbs are healthy. They possess antioxidant, anti-inflammatory, antitumorigenic, anticarcinogenic, and glucose- and cholesterol-lowering benefits as well as properties that positively affect cognition and mood. Frequent consumption of spicy foods is linked to a lower risk of death from cancer and ischemic heart and respiratory system diseases. (Jiang, 2019)

3. They are open to experimenting with new flavors and cuisines.

Gen Z is the most ethnically diverse generation - 48% are non-white. (Fry & Parker, 2018) Perhaps that is part of the reason why 79% of Gen Z eats "specialty foods" and 42% say they favor "street food." (Newhart, 2019)

Next Steps

Pending approval of this recommendation, we will begin exploring media opportunities and developing a creative brief.

2018 American Community Survey. *census.gov.* Retrieved May 13, 2020, from https://data.census.gov/cedsci/all?t=Age%20and%20Sex&tid=ACSST1Y2018.S0101&hidePreview=false

Davis, D. (2020, January 28) Gen Zers have a spending power of over $140 billion, and it's driving the frenzy of retailers and brands trying to win their dollars. *businessinsider.com.* Retrieved May 13, 2020, from https://www.businessinsider.com/retail-courts-gen-z-spending-power-over-140-billion-2020-1

Valdez, K. (2018, January) Why Now is the Time for Restaurants to Court Gen Z. *qsrmagazine.com.* Retrieved May 11, 2020, from https://www.qsrmagazine.com/outside-insights/why-now-time-restaurants-court-gen-z

(2017. December 4) The Majority of 18-24-Year-Olds Live in Their Parents' Home, As Do 1 in 6 Older Millennials. *marketingcharts.com.* Retrieved May 13, 2020, from https://www.marketingcharts.com/demographics-and-audiences-81471

Valdez, K. (2018, January) Why Now is the Time for Restaurants to Court Gen Z. *qsrmagazine.com.* Retrieved May 11, 2020, from https://www.qsrmagazine.com/outside-insights/why-now-time-restaurants-court-gen-z

Granderson, D. (2019, February 11) Gen Z Adults Seek Foods Fitting Their Busy, Yet Health Conscious Lifestyles. *prnewswire.com* Retrieved May 8, 2020, from https://www.prnewswire.com/news-releases/gen-z-adults-seek-foods-fitting-their-busy-yet-health-conscious-lifestyles-300793417.html

(2020, April 24) How Restaurants Can Please the Members of Generation Z. *aaronallen.com* Retrieved May 8, 2020, from https://aaronallen.com/blog/gen-z-food-trends

Sloan, A. (2019, July 1) Demographic Disrupters. *ift.org.* Retrieved May 8, 2020, from https://www.ift.org/news-and-publications/food-technology-magazine/issues/2019/july/features/food-purchasing-and-consumption-generalization-preferences

Fry, R. & Parker, K. (2018, November 15) Early Benchmarks Show 'Post-Millennials' on Track to Be Most Diverse, Best-Educated Generation Yet. *pewresearch.org.* Retrieved May 11, 2020, from https://www.pewsocialtrends.org/2018/11/15/early-benchmarks-show-post-millennials-on-track-to-be-most-diverse-best-educated-generation-yet/

Jiang, T. (2019, March 1) Health Benefits of Culinary Herbs and Spices. *nih.gov.* Retrieved March 10, 2020, from https://www.ncbi.nlm.nih.gov/pubmed/30651162

Newhart, B. (2019, January 22) Shopping small: 79% of Gen Z buys specialty foods. *beveragedaily.com.* Retrieved May 11, 2020, from https://www.beveragedaily.com/Article/2019/01/22/Shopping-small-79-of-Gen-Z-buys-specialty-foods

Part 2
What you say (message)

Chapter 5. Emotions

All decisions are emotional and money doesn't buy happiness.

Richard Thaler's research referenced in the Preface is just one example of the body of research that has been done in the past few decades which led to our understanding that all decisions are emotional.

We decide emotionally and justify rationally. You didn't buy that BMW because it makes you feel important - you bought it because it gets good gas mileage. (Remember, most lies are told to preserve self-esteem.)

Research shows that our strongest memories are those that are associated with emotion. Long-term memories are influenced by the emotion experienced during the event as well as by the emotion experienced when thinking about it later.[1]

Emotional events are often remembered with greater accuracy and vividness. Emotion can enhance memory for details, including the color of the font in which a word was presented, the spatial location of a word on a computer screen, or whether information was visually presented or mentally imagined.

Negative emotions enhance memory accuracy more than positive emotions. Since the primary function of emotion is to guide action and plan for future occurrences, it makes sense that attention would be more focused on potentially threatening information and memory mechanisms would ensure those details would be remembered.[2]

Integral emotions arise from the choice at hand. Examples include someone deciding to drive because they are afraid to fly. Or making less risky decisions during a time of anxiety.

Incidental emotions are unrelated to the choice at hand, but are just as powerful if not more. They are how we feel - what kind of mood we are in. For instance, research shows that the stock market performs better on sunny days and domestic violence increases when the home team loses. That's why it is important to pick your moment carefully when you are trying to persuade.[3]

Bad versus Good

Bad is stronger than good. That's the actual title of a seminal research study. As the name implies, the greater power of bad events over good ones is pervasive. Bad emotions have more impact than good ones. Bad information is processed more thoroughly than good. Bad impressions and stereotypes are quicker to form and more resistant to change. And, we are more motivated to avoid bad self-definitions than to achieve good ones.[4]

We fear change because we think it will be bad. While the status quo may not be optimal it is predictable. Change is not. So we project negatively and assume that things we will be worse after than they were before. To make change palatable it needs to be small enough to fit within our zone of acceptance - close enough to our existing beliefs that it will be considered, easy enough to be incorporated without major upset.[5]

We fear losing more than we enjoy winning and would be more upset to lose $50 than we would be to gain $50. We call this loss aversion. And it is a major factor in decision-making. Research shows that a loss hurts twice as much as a gain of the same size.[6] We act accordingly.

To take advantage of this emotion, marketers create scarcity. How? Deadlines (sale ends today), limited numbers (only 25 available), limited access (members only), potential loss (You could already be a winner) and restricted freedom ("sold" signs) are all examples of this principle in action.[7]

Broadway shows have recognized this behavior and have capitalized on it by publicizing the impending closure of shows. As a result, many have earned significant sums in their final weeks. Who goes at the last minute? Some of the attendees are those who have put off going, while others decide to see the show again before it closes.

Using this strategy in 2019, the *Cher Show* was able to earn $1 million in its final week, up $200K from the previous week. It was the first time in three months that the show crossed the seven figure mark.[8]

Loss aversion also impacts the way people respond to rewards. In one experiment, employees were paid to lose weight. When they were offered $1.40 a day for each day they walked 7000 steps, participants met the goal 35% of the time. But when they started out the month with $42, and lost $1.40 each day they failed to meet goal, 45% of the time the goal was met.[9] Because we hate to lose more than we like to win.

Clearly incentives can be tricky. Sometimes penalties can backfire. When daycare centers began fining parents for late pickups, tardiness increased. Apparently parents believed that they were purchasing "lateness" with their fines.[10]

And rewards can backfire too. In a study of over 15,000 middle and high school students, handing out awards for excellent attendance resulted in a decline in attendance. Students who received a surprise award for past attendance had 8.3% more absences in the following month. When the students were told in advance about the awards, absences increased by 8.9% in the following month.

Why? Perhaps providing an extrinsic motivation depresses internal motivation. The awards also created a benchmark for students to measure themselves versus their peers. And, it signaled that their performance exceeded expectations, giving them a license to take a break. All very rational reasons.

But then the researchers go on to say - it may also be that they reduced their performance to match those of their friends in order to maintain group harmony. In other words, they stepped down their performance to conform to tribal norms.[11]

Research about getting people to use stronger passwords showed that a powerful incentive like letting people keep their passwords longer if they are stronger, works best if it is helped a bit by nudges. Specifically as the password is created, feedback about both its strength and how long the person would be allowed to use it, proved to be persuasive.[12]

Measles

Because bad impressions are more resistant to change, fear seems to be one of the few strategies that can counter them. Case in point, the misconceptions about vaccinations and autism has led many Americans to refuse to vaccinate their children. As a result, measles an eradicated disease, is on the rise.

In a study parents were exposed to either:
1. research showing that vaccines do not cause autism
2. some unrelated scientific vignettes
3. photos of infected children, with a paragraph written by the worried parent.

Only the last approach had an effect. It uses fear (bad is stronger than good) and visuals, which evoke more emotions and are more memorable than words. The thoughts from the worried parent stimulate empathy and are meant to create provincial norms, i.e. if you are worried like this parent, here's what you need to do.[13]

Happiness

Our emotions not only serve to remind us of things we want to avoid, but also things we want to repeat, or perhaps try for the first time because they look so appealing on social media. But in fact we are often mistaken about what truly brings us joy. Here's what the research says.

Meeting Challenges

Research shows that what makes us happy is to set goals for ourselves and then achieve them. The best goals have intermediate points so that we can measure our progress as we go. Once we achieve our goals, we need to start over again with a new challenge.[14]

The more difficult and valued a goal is, the more intense our efforts will be to attain it, and the happier we will feel when we succeed. The experience of success generates positive emotions and an increase in confidence, while the capacity to plan for the future positively impacts perceived control over outcomes.[15]

Experiences versus Things

People who use their money to buy experiences are happier than people who use their money to buy things. One reason is tied to memory. Once you buy a product it begins to depreciate in value thanks to ongoing usage and associated wear and tear. But with experiences, the opposite happens. After a few weeks, you forget about the terrible plane flight and only remember how wonderful the trip was.[16]

Beyond this, research has also shown that shared experiences allow us to connect more deeply with others. And that while it is clear that some people achieve sense of self through what they buy, most of us are not the sum total of our possessions. Rather we are the result of our collective experiences.

Finally, experiences are measured and valued on their own terms without comparison to other experiences.[17] Ah yes, to quote Theodore Roosevelt , "Comparison is the thief of joy."[18]

Interestingly, this is one of those areas where social class makes a difference. Studies have shown that lower income classes still favor the purchasing of things over experiences. According to researchers, this is because people with more resources can afford to spend money on self-development and self-expression, while those with fewer resources are more likely to be concerned about making financially wise purchases.[19]

That sounds rational. But we know that decision-making isn't. So perhaps what's really going on here is an example of "positional concerns" i.e. trying to one up one's friends, and that the ultimate goal behind both purchases is the same -- to impress others. Lower income people do that by buying a fancy car or sneakers, while upper income people take a trip to Machu Picchu. Looking at social media we see people brag about their latest adventures on Facebook the same way they once showed off their $4,000 pocketbooks.

There also appears to be an age skew to experiential purchases with 78% of Millennials saying that they would choose to spend money on an experience or event rather than a thing. Perhaps it's because some of their best memories are from experiences (77%) or perhaps the 69% of Millennials who admit it's all about FOMO (fear of missing out) are more accurate.[20]

But it could be as simple as having less money to spend on things, or greater difficulty making decisions about which things to buy. Or perhaps in a world that is more and more about virtual interactions, it's the desire to have a real world experience instead.

Recognizing the power of the experience, Vergenoegd Wine in South Africa touted the fact that to keep their vineyards snail and pest free they relied on ducks rather than chemicals. They began scheduling duck parades for visitors, added the birds to the farm's logo and highlighted them on the website. The result? Sales doubled in less than a year.[21]

Meanwhile, with research showing that an unexpected free dessert can increase staff tips by 18%[22], even upscale restaurants like Tocqueville, where a eight-course meal costs $175, are raising the bar on the experience by sending diners home with a half dozen of pale blue heritage eggs.[23]

Anticipation is underrated

Depending upon your family traditions you may remember looking at those gift wrapped packages under the tree and wondering what was in them. Did you shake them? Sure you did.

Research shows that subjects receiving a gift-wrapped item had a more favorable attitude toward owning it than those who received an unwrapped item. It appears that this is due to the fact that wrapped gifts are associated with happy occasions.[24]

But even transparent wrapping can have a positive effect on mood because wrapping slows down the opening process which helps us to pay attention to the experience.[25]

Since unwrapping gifts makes us happy, is it any wonder then that unboxing videos on YouTube are very popular? In 2019, You Tube's top earner was an eight year old boy named Ryan Kaji. His channel - *Ryan ToysReview*, devoted to unboxing - had 23 million subscribers. He earned over $20 million.[26]

Money doesn't buy happiness

Studies show that while money does not buy happiness, the lack of money can buy unhappiness. The cut-off point seems to be ~ $75K. At that point more money will not make you much happier, even if you think it will. In fact, people thought that increasing their income from $25K to $55K would double their satisfaction. Instead their happiness increased by only 9%.[27]

But what you do with your money can buy happiness. For instance, research has shown that using money to buy time makes people happier.

So the decision to take a taxi instead of a bus, or having dinner delivered instead of cooking, does result in greater happiness. While a 2017 global study showed that only 28% of people were using money in this way, those that did showed greater life satisfaction. Why? Because buying time alleviates the negative effect of time pressure. Outsourcing cooking, shopping and household maintenance allows individuals the opportunity to spend more time doing things that they enjoy.[28]

More sex might buy happiness

If you are single , or in a bad relationship, you need to earn $100K more each year to be as happy as a happily married person. If you have sex just once a month, you'd need to earn $50,000 more a year to be as happy as someone having sex once a week with a monogamous partner.[29]

So does that mean you should simply have more sex? Not so fast. In a study where couples were asked to double the frequency of their encounters they were not happier. In fact, their energy and enthusiasm declined as did the quality of their sex. The happiness comes from having the right amount of sex as determined by the couples.[30]

But if you are wondering how often Americans really have sex, a statistician looked at population, pregnancies and condom usage and determined that on average Americans are having sex every 12 days. It's a good reminder of how people lie to protect their self esteem, and why hard data is more accurate than surveys.[31]

Helping others

Global research shows that in 120 out of 136 countries there is a positive relationship between giving and happiness. Why? Giving satisfies the need for social connection. And assuming people have control over who they give to and how they give, they will feel a personal sense of accomplishment as well when they give to others.[32]

But it is important to note that we only feel this way when we help others who we perceive to be like ourselves. Yes, empathy bias is real. Multiple studies on Israelis and Palestinians reveal that people who engage in extreme violence do not necessarily lack empathy. Instead, they have high empathy for the group they belong to and low empathy for the group they oppose. It's that tribe thing again.[33]

In NYC, a reporter who spent a week as a delivery person noted that 2/3 of his customers did not tip. Who tipped most of the time? - people who lived in public housing. Who rarely tipped? - NYU students. Why were those of lesser means more likely to tip? Perhaps because they believed the delivery people were part of their tribe.[34]

We are also more responsive to individuals in need, rather than groups. That's why fund raising campaigns for Unicef typically feature an individual, very adorable child.

It also works for dogs. A commercial for Pedigree's adoption campaign featured a shelter dog named Oliver who was seeking a home. People became so invested in Oliver that the company needed to air a follow-up ad showing him living happily ever after in his new home to satisfy viewers.[35]

The campaign not only raised millions for Pedigree's non-profit foundation, it also increased dog food sales - so much so that the company even decided to air the campaign on the

Super Bowl in 2009. When asked if they intended to shift their strategy for the occasion to something more product-focused, they replied "Every time we run this campaign, we see increased sales." That's the power of cause marketing.[36]

Having More Friends

A study published in the *British Journal of Psychology* looked at 15,000 respondents and found that people who had more social interactions with close friends reported being happier. With one exception. People with high I.Q.s who were pursuing a long-term goal were happier spending less time with others, presumably so that they could spend more time on their projects.[37] It's another circumstance where the small print on the data matters.

Getting Older

Happiness generally rises with age. Not that any age group seems to be particularly happy. Rates over the past five decades ranged from a high of 47% among 65+ in 1984 to a low of 26% for 18-34 year-olds in 1994. Over the past five decades it appears that all age groups are less happy. Even the happiest in the 65+ age group dropped from a high of 47% in 1984 to a low of 36% in 2014.[38]

Perhaps the increase in social media is fueling this trend as we see others apparently living much happier lives than we do. This would be consistent with the research that shows an increase in isolation and loneliness among heavy users of social media.[39]

Or it could be that we are watching too much tv. Women now spend 15% of their waking hours watching tv, while men spend 17% of theirs. Research shows that watching television increases serotonin and therefore may provide some short-term stress relief. But it does not appear to be as successful as other more engaging activities - such as visiting friends, exercising, attending church, playing/listening to music, fishing, reading a book, and painting, knitting or crafting are in increasing happiness.[40]

Values

Research has shown that values vary widely based on social class. This is a reflection of different life experiences. Less affluent people rely more on family and friends. When a low income person moves, their friends help them. When an upper income person moves, they hire someone to help them.

As a result of these realities the different groups teach their children different values. So working class folks favor values that bind communities together like solidarity and loyalty. While elites focus on personal achievement and individuality - values that will help them to earn more money.[41]

We also see different values for different generations. These too are rooted in different life experiences. Is it any wonder that the Silent Generation - who served in WWII and Korea have different thoughts about patriotism than Millennials?[42]

People are increasingly interested in using brands that reflect their personal values. In a 2019 survey by Edelman, nearly 60% of consumers said that they would "choose, switch, avoid or boycott a brand based on its stand on societal issues, up from 47% in 2017."[43]

And why not? It's one way to decide between product A or B, when the differences between the product are in fact very slight. If you decide not to use L.L. Bean anymore because of the illegal contributions Linda Bean made to the Trump campaign[44], you can easily switch to Patagonia who has a stellar environmental record and a female CEO.[45]

Levi's

After two decades of net losses and poor growth Levi's made a comeback, and hit a sales record in 2017. How did they do it? They attribute their success to cause marketing.

It all started in 2016 when a customer in a dressing room at a Levi's store in Atlanta accidentally shot himself while trying on jeans. The company decided to publish an open letter asking customers not to carry guns while they shop. And they backed it up with a $1 million fund supporting organizations focused on gun safety. Cue the hate mail.[46]

But sales went up 11% in the following quarter, the fourth quarter in a row of double-digit revenue gains. So the company doubled down and took a stand against climate change too.[47]

The "wash less" campaign kicked off in January 2018 with media appearances by CEO Chip Bergh encouraging people not to wash their jeans. It ignited a powerful debate.[48] The Levi's product label, which reads - "Care for our planet: Wash less, wash cold, line dry, donate or recycle," makes it very clear where the company stands.

Meanwhile in a perfect example of unintended consequences, these positions led to a 3% increase in support for Levi's among Democrats. But also a 13% increase in Republicans buying Wranglers, as each party followed the dictates of its tribe. In case you are wondering, Levi's is the top brand in the category with 12% of sales in 2018, versus 4.8% for Wranglers, the number two brand.

Partisan divides can now be found not only in cable news preferences (CNN for Democrats, Fox for Republicans) but also car brands - VW for Democrats, GMC for Republicans, sports - NBA for Democrats and NASCAR for Republicans, and chain stores where Democrats prefer Starbucks while Republicans prefer Chick-fil-A.[49]

The strength of the tribe has never been clearer.

Chapter 6. Personality types

Communication preferences are influenced by personality type.

There are several personality typing systems being used today. The most widely used is Myers-Briggs (MBTI). Since it is a useful tool in understanding human behavior, we will review some of its key points. But bear in mind, that it is most useful when you take the test yourself (preferably the full print version) and read all of the background information that is provided.

Here's a link in case you would like to do that... https://www.mbtionline.com/?utm_source=MBF&utm_medium=link&utm_campaign=online

MBTI was developed by Katherine Briggs and Isabel Briggs-Myers in 1943, based on Carl Jung's research to help explain behavioral differences in healthy people. The system looks at personality based on four continuums. These are:

1. How we are energized.
Extroversion (E) vs. Introversion (I).

How do you like to learn? Do you think out loud and prefer discussions and debate? Then your preference veers toward Extroversion. If you would rather think first and then speak, your preference is for Introversion.

2. What type of information we trust.
Sensing (S) vs. Intuition (N).

Do you rely on facts? Prefer to deal with what is known and familiar? Focus on what is rather than what might be? Then your preference is for Sensing. If you ask lots of questions, and always want to know the reason why, then you preference is for Intuition.

3. Our approach to decision-making.
Thinking (T) vs. Feeling (F).

Do you prefer logical analysis? Do you strive to be fair? Do you remain detached from the outcome of your decisions? If so, then your preference is for Thinking. If you care more about people and values, and prioritize harmony and compassion then your preference is for Feeling.

4. How we live our lives.
Judging (J) vs. Perceiving (P).

Are you organized, methodical and decisive? Then your preference is for Judging. If you are more spontaneous and flexible, then your preference is for Perceiving.

Where you fall within the spectrum matters. A very strong "J" will behave quite differently from a moderate one. But even if we just look at the 16 different preference groups without worrying about nuance, we can learn much about human behavior.

The first thing to note is that the largest group (ISFJ) represents about 13.8% of the US population, while the smallest (INFJ) accounts for a mere 1.5%. That means the odds that you are dealing with someone just like you are very slim.

MBTI has developed U.S. norms and these show that while the population is fairly close to evenly split between "E's" and "I's" - 49.3% versus 50.7%, the same is not true for some of the other measures.[1]

When we look at task people (T) versus relationship people (F) we see a 40.2%/59.8% split in favor of relationships. This explains why referrals from friends and storytelling are such successful marketing techniques. These folks also respond well to user testimonials.

Planners (J) represent 54.1% of the population, while the spontaneous (P) represent 45.9%. So it's interesting that Hotwire has observed that more than half of their bookings are made within 0-2 days before the trip - slightly more than we would expect.[2]

But we see the largest difference in preferences when we look at the spectrum which addresses the type of information that we trust. "S's" those that operate in the here and now represent a whopping 73.3% of the population versus 26.7% for the what if's (N).

Additional research has shown that S's are more influenced by the attractiveness of product endorsers - think celebrities. They are also more influenced by conformity cues - e.g. "most popular" and "best seller" lists. And they are relatively unaffected by argument quality - so you can skip the body copy.[3]

N's on the other hand, process arguments more extensively even when product evaluation is not a goal - they like to know why and are more likely to respond to longer form arguments such as editorials. Not surprisingly, they are more influenced by authority figures than they are by celebrities.[4]

There is a vast amount of additional research available based on MBTI. Some has unearthed differences between genders and cultures. Yet, law enforcement officers in Australia, the United Kingdom, and the U.S. all show preferences for ISTJ and ESTJ profiles.[5]

That having been said, given the heavy skew toward "S's" in the population, marketing efforts are likely to be more successful if they focus on "S" communication preferences. Additional information could be made available, perhaps in a different medium, for "N's," sincc wc know that they will seek the information out on their own.

Chapter 7. Decision-making

It's hard to make decisions, so we use shortcuts.

Decision-making is tough. It tires our minds the same way that exercise tires our bodies. The more options there are, the more difficult the decision. The more choices you make throughout the day, the harder each one becomes. It's a cumulative effect.[1]

Anyone who has renovated a home, or planned a wedding knows this. As someone once said - "Who knew there could be so many shades of blue?"

Car dealers do. Decision-fatigue is their friend. That's why after asking customers to make numerous decisions about models, colors and finishes, they casually ask -- would you like an extended warranty? At that point, we usually say yes even though they don't make financial sense.

Having more choices makes choosing more difficult, because it means more chances to make a mistake. Ah, yes - loss aversion. I remember a time when my parents went to a store to buy soda and came back empty handed due to "analysis paralysis" because there were too many choices.

Recognizing this, many new online start-ups are offering "curated" selections of items, i.e. fewer choices. Examples include Great Jones. They offer only five pieces of cookware in five trendy matte colors suitable for Instagram posts - blueberry, broccoli, earl grey, mustard and macaron (better known as pink.) Just what Millennials are looking for.[2]

Eyeglasses, mattresses, linens and razors are among the other products playing in the space of "good enough" choices.

It's a trend that's probably here to stay. Because Millennials are desperately afraid of making the wrong choice.

Being raised by helicopter parents in an era of participation trophies has created a generation that has never experienced failure personally and therefore hasn't learned how to bounce back from it. It's a shame as it is well established that we learn more from our failures than we do from our successes. But the immediate result is that many Millennials are unable to make choices without crowd-sourcing opinions first.

They are also starting fewer businesses. The percentage of people under 30 who own their business has fallen from 10.6% to 3.6%, a 24-year low. And 41% admit that it is fear of failure that is holding them back.[3]

Once decision fatigue sets in, we start looking for shortcuts - ways to make decisions with less effort. Let's look at some of the most common ones.

Easy

People tend to follow the course of action that requires the least amount of effort. Most of the time we are willing to settle for good enough and move on. Consider this, when was the last time you read an entire restaurant menu?

When we choose a recommended option, we are enlisting the aid of experts. When we phone a friend and ask their opinion, we are using word-of-mouth. And when we do nothing, like choosing not to vote, we are simply allowing others to decide for us.[4]

One wonders how much the urge to avoid decision-making is due to fear of choosing incorrectly. In Austria where organ donations are "opt-out," 90% donate. In the U.S. where organ donations are "opt-in" only 15% donate. Could Austrians possibly be that more altruistic than Americans? Or is it all about framing?

It's likely that the act of opting-in makes donating seem like a more substantial commitment than opting-out does. In fact in the U.S., donating an organ was thought to be roughly equivalent to giving away half of one's wealth to charity upon one's death. But in opt-in countries, it fell between letting others get ahead of one in line and volunteering to help the poor. A very different mindset indeed.[5]

We pay more attention to information that is easily available, and favor information that reinforces our beliefs (confirmation bias), while ignoring information that doesn't (selective perception).[6]

We make decisions easier by reducing our decision criteria to one dimension. Common criteria include price, quality, and availability. Interestingly a low price product can be seen as a bargain or poor quality. It's all about the interpretation.[7]

Talking about a brand's longevity and heritage can provide both quality reassurance and evoke a positive emotional resonance because it activates nostalgia. But it is important to note that this approach is likely to be more successful with "N's" and "T's" both of whom are in the minority when compared to "S's" and "F's."[8]

Reducing the number of choices also makes decisions easier. Mark Zuckerberg wears the same thing every day, as did Steve Jobs. And when he was in office, President Obama wore only grey or blue suits and ate the same thing for breakfast every day, so he could save his energy for important decisions.[9]

Social Proof

This is another way of saying "let someone else decide for you." When people are unsure about what to do they will often follow others, looking for the wisdom of the crowd to aid their decisions. We call this informational conformity.[10]

It's easy to see why people take comfort in going with the crowd. It's an evolutionary based choice - those that stayed with the tribe were more likely to survive. But the tendency lingers even if the physical imperative is no longer driving it.

Beyond this, we are all social creatures with a great need to belong. Some more than others. "F" personality types (who are the majority) in particular seek close social ties. Remember, Myers-Briggs describes them as people who "strive for harmony and positive interactions."[11]

Therefore we often practice conformity in order to belong to a group, changing behavior to match theirs even if we do not agree with them. In fact, research tells us that 2/3 of people will conform in public.[12]

And that "S" personalities - and therefore the majority of Americans, prefer to follow the crowd, hence the success of top ten lists. Not to mention peer pressure.[13]

In one example, telling people that a fundraising goal was to get nine people to donate and that eight already had, increased the percentage of people donating from 49% to 55%. Being told you are the person who can put a fundraiser over the top is a powerful motivator, and clearly it isn't only about peer pressure.[14]

On the other hand, when people see their peers behaving in inappropriate ways they often adapt their behavior to match the group norm. How to prevent this from happening? Prosecute the criminals and make an example of them. Research on crime has shown that it is the likelihood of getting caught that is the best deterrence for both the criminals and their peers.[15]

Hence the perp walks just before the yearly IRS filing deadline. Shame can be a powerful motivator too.[16]

The desire to conform is not always a bad thing. We have found that peer pressure can be used successfully to change negative behavior. Monthly emails informing doctors about how their rate of antibiotic prescriptions compares to those of other doctors has proved to be an effective tool for reducing prescriptions. The emails identified "top performers" and included a personalized account of unnecessary prescriptions by the doctor versus the count for a typical top performer. Using this methodology inappropriate prescribing dropped from 19.9% to 3.7%.[17]

Positional Concerns

The flip side of social proof is "positional concerns" which involves our tendency to measure ourselves via comparisons. Not surprisingly, how an individual feels they are doing is typically affected more by earnings relative to others than absolute wealth.

In fact, H.L. Mencken defined wealth as "any income that is at least $100 more a year than the income of one's wife's sister's husband."[18]

Since high standing in a society can yield respect admiration and power, people will seek to convince others of their greater wealth, even if this means lying. And, it's the reason why a majority of people will actually be happier making less money as long as they are still making more money than their friends.[19]

Finally, new research shows that when it comes to envy, we are more jealous of our friends' future plans than we are of their past adventures. It seems the brain has evolved to have an emotional bias toward the future. First we decide what we want and then we figure out how to get it. Someone else's plans stimulate both bad feelings - envy, but also positive ones - a desire to get what our friends have. The latter feelings linger even while envy abates.[20]

Reciprocity

"Nothing is more costly than something given free of charge"
- Japanese saying

There is no such thing as a free lunch. That trial membership at the gym is meant to persuade you to sign up. And if it's opt-out you may end up with a six month membership due to inertia. Victoria's Secret is willing to give you free underwear because they are betting that once you are in the store you will buy more than just the undies.

Interestingly, one of the most effective "free" things someone can offer is sharing a secret, e.g., "off the record..." Sharing information that is not widely known creates a sense of intimacy and makes the listener feel important.[21]

Reciprocity usually involves quid pro quo rather than freebies. Someone gives you something and you return the gesture, because people are more likely to return favors in response to those given to them. So when someone offers you a 15% discount in return for your email address they are counting on you to consider it a fair deal and respond positively.

But obligation can be part of the equation too. When charities send you personalized address labels with their fundraising requests, they are hoping that you will feel obligated to contribute. And they may be right. Donations increase from 18% to 35% when labels are included.[22]

Consistency

Once we have devoted energy to something, we are more likely to continue doing it, because we don't want what we have already done to go to waste. For example, if you spent two hours researching lamps online and aren't convinced you have found the best option yet, you have two choices. You can invest more time, or walk away. Most people will choose to invest more time.[23]

Loyalty programs are a way to capitalize on this behavior. Even having a "most bought" list can be enough of an advantage to cultivate future sales.

Finally, if you donate to a charity once you are more likely to do it again. You are also more likely to donate to a similar cause. That's why non-profits share contact information.

Social Causes

As discussed in chapter five, people want to use brands that share their values. This is particularly true of younger generations. 83% of Millennials say that it is important to them that the companies they buy from align with their values. Only 73% of Gen X agree and 60% of Baby Boomers.

About two-thirds (65%) of Millennials say they have boycotted a brand that took the opposing stance on an issue, and 62% favor products that show off their political and social beliefs. Again older generations appear to be less motivated by social causes with only 21% of Boomers favoring products that express their political and social beliefs.[24]

<u>Nike</u>
Perhaps one of the most interesting examples of value-based marketing today is Nike's support of Colin Kaepernick.

In 2016, Kaepernick took a knee for equality at an NFL game and became an iconic activist. The NFL rushed to distance themselves from him immediately and he has yet to be rehired. But when the "Black Lives Matter" movement reached a tipping point in June 2020, Roger Goodell, the Commissioner of the NFL, began "encouraging" teams to sign him.[25]

In the meantime, Nike, who clearly has a handle on their consumers' values hired Kaepernick to be their spokesperson. Why? Because 66% of consumers say it's important for brands to take public stands on social and political issues, and 60% of Millennials are belief-driven buyers.

So the company wasn't worried about boycott calls from non-users like Mitch McConnell. Why would they be? As Matt Powell noted, "Old angry white guys are not a core demographic for Nike."

And in a poll about knelling during the national anthem, 63% of people over 50 said it was never appropriate, while only 38% of people under 30 agreed.[26]

Guess who buys more sneakers? Is it any wonder that Nike's sales responded positively to their alliance with Kaepernick and rose 10% in the quarter after the campaign began airing?[27]

And the continuing partnership, which included a custom shoe in 2019, no doubt contributed to a 10% increase in sales in the final quarter of 2019, and a 36% increase in stock prices for the year.[28]

Note that, there are two factors at work here - the desire to support ones values and the fact that values differ by age. Let's also not forget that it is easier for a company to support a cause then it is for them to fix their customer service issues, or whatever else is vexing them. And given the proliferation of products with no clear differentiation and these latest stats about value based buying, more and more companies are heading in that direction.

Likeability

A study by *The Advertising Research Foundation* concluded that "likeability" is the measure that is most predictive of whether or not an advertisement will increase brand sales. Additional research found that emotional response to a television commercial can increase intent to buy a product by a factor of 3-to-1. For a print ad, it's 2-to-1.[29]

Why? Because 59.8% of Americans (F's) care more about relationships than tasks. Therefore it stands to reason that they would be more easily persuaded by people that they like, since their ultimate goal is to enhance the relationship.

This is why Etsy advises its entrepreneurs to connect with customers by sharing something personal like photos of their kids or stories about their projects.[30]

Celebrity presenters have a dual appeal because not only do people like them, 73.3% of Americans (S's) are swayed by the attractiveness of the presenter.

In 2014, Lincoln hired Matthew McConaughey as a spokesperson for the Lincoln MKC. As a result, they had their best October in seven years, 2014 sales increased by 15.6% versus previous year and sales were up 25% since 2013. Why? Because people like Matt. They told the dealers as much when they were buying their cars. To quote one, "people come in here and say, 'Oh, he's my favorite actor, he's just wonderful.' " And "they talk more about Matt than the car."[31]

In 2016, Beyonce preformed *Formation* at The Super Bowl, and Red Lobster sales went up by 33%.[32]

If you aren't a celebrity, demonstrating similarity, which encourages liking, can increase the probability that a message will be well received. Once again, it comes down to whether or not they believe that you belong to the same tribe. And, if a listener believes that the person sending the message is "someone like me" they might even be open to a contrary point of view.[33]

Attractiveness

But being pretty also matters because thanks to the halo effect, we think that prettier people are also smarter, funnier and more likable. Is it any surprise then that professors awarded a chili pepper on RateMyProfessors.com had higher overall teaching scores? Or that the chili pepper rating was dropped in 2018?[34]

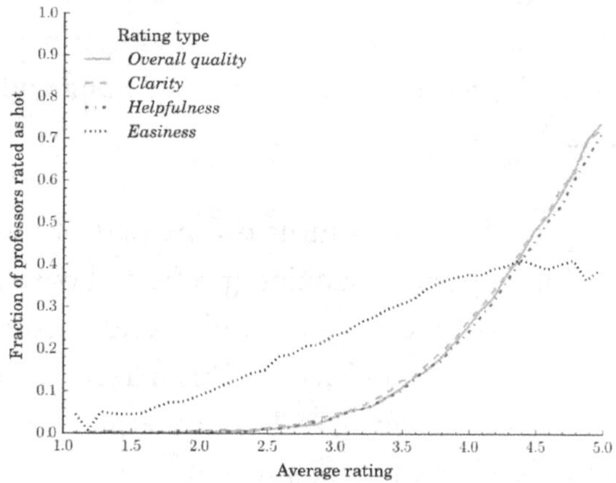

Figure 3. Plot of the fraction of professors rated as 'hot' as a function of average rating, which includes *overall quality* (solid line), *clarity* (dashed line), *helpfulness* (dot-dashed line) and *easiness* (dotted line).

Probably not. But it might be a surprise to discover that students learn more from teachers they find attractive. The students believe they are more motivating, easier to follow and possessed of greater health, intelligence and competence. As a result, student performance goes up by about half a letter grade.[35]

Stress

People make poorer decisions when they are stressed. We use memories of our past decisions - especially those that were bad, to make future decisions that are good. Chronic stress impairs the memory consolidation and retrieval that we rely on for doing that properly. Therefore when making decisions under stress we are more likely to frame the issue incorrectly and fail to consider all viable options.

There is also a direct link between stress exposure and changes in loss-aversion patterns. So we see stressed individuals display increased levels of risk taking and making risky choices.[36]

By increasing cortisol, stress turns off the part of the brain responsible for long-term planning (prefrontal cortex). And activates the parts of the brain (amygdala and striatum) linked to the tendency to act impulsively. This makes people more likely to eat candy, ice cream, and any other number of unhealthy foods when they are stressed.[37]

Yet another example of poor decision-making under stress

Chapter 8. Consumer insights

The emotional hook.

In the mid-90's when research about the role of emotions in decision-making first started to emerge, people realized that successful marketing was more about the person who was buying the brand than it was about the brand. So, research people morphed into strategic planners, and we began looking for consumer insights.

A consumer insight is something that the target thinks or feels that we can use to make an emotional connection with them. It is the way we take the relevant psychological, sociological and anthropological data and incorporate it into marketing strategy.

Dove

In 2006, Dove began its much heralded, Effie award winning, Real Beauty campaign. The campaign, which features women who are not quite as perfect as those we typically see in mass communications touched a nerve.

After its launch, the brand experienced two years of double-digit sales growth. The campaign strengthened brand loyalty among existing customers, resulting in a greater number of current users buying more than one product, and increased share growth in four of its five major categories.[1]

The consumer insight that led to its development was: "Only two percent of women consider themselves beautiful" - a fact that was uncovered in a global survey. In a subsequent update, the percentage has increased to four percent.[2] Not much of an improvement.

Let's go back to the target definitions from chapter two and add a consumer insight...

Women (gender) 18-24 (age range) who want to meet someone (plus one), but hate the bar scene (consumer insight)

Women (gender) 18-24 (age range) who think a new look might help them get more dates (plus one), but are intimidated by cosmetic counters (consumer insight)

Men (gender) 45-60 (age range) who enjoy mountain biking (plus one) and want to explore far flung locations (consumer insight)

Dads (gender) 24-39 with kids under 18 (age range), who are cooking more so their families will be healthier (plus one) and want to be super heroes (consumer insight)

Women (gender) 23-33 (age range) who care about the environment because they enjoy outdoor sports (plus one) and want to support brands who share their values (consumer insight)

Men (gender) 18-24 (age range) who want to eat healthier (plus one) but don't cook (consumer insight)

You can see how at this point your target definition is robust enough to yield superior communications.

Chapter 9. Positioning Statements

They're the best format for research.

While there are many ways to express strategies, one of the most common and most useful is the positioning statement.

A positioning statement summarizes the key elements of the strategy and puts them into one long, run-on sentence. It is extremely helpful in articulating a brand's strategy and achieving consensus for it among key constituents. It is also the best format for testing because it removes all executional elements from the equation and forces people to focus only on the proposition being expressed.

While formats vary slightly, the one below captures all the essential elements.

Positioning Statement Format

To ___*(target market: gender, age range, plus one)*___,

and/but ___*(consumer insight)*___,

Brand XYZ ___*(product or service)*___,

is ___*(key message)*___,

because ___*(three reasons to believe)*___.

Here is an example of a positioning statement for a B-to-B telecom service.

To Men (gender) 25-35 (age range), who are IT Professionals (plus one), Company X understands your need to stay connected and be informed (consumer insight), that's why we're introducing Premium Plus Service (brand), a revolutionary breakthrough in integrated communications (key message)—a single network of virtually unlimited capacity that will enable high-speed online access (reason 1), video applications (reason 2), and multiple simultaneous telephone services (reason 3) so you can communicate in ways that have never been feasible before.

Note that research indicates that we have become so accustomed to the use of the word "because" prior to the presentation of rationale for the claim preceding it, that using this argument structure makes the claim more credible regardless of the support provided.[1]

This positioning statement was one of several developed and then tested to see which one was the most salient. When we tested them, we were concerned that they had become too long, so we included an option that did not provide reasons to believe, and, instead, ended after the key message. Consistent with the research, it did not test as well.

Here's a positioning statement for Gen X dads.

To Dads (gender) 24-39 with kids under 18 (age range), who are cooking more so their families will be healthier (plus one) and want to be super heroes (consumer insight), McCormick spices (brand) are the perfect ingredients for the meals they cook (key message), because they have more disease-fighting antioxidants than most fruits and vegetables (reason 1), McCormick provides "flavor print" information so they can decide which spices to use (reason 2), and the "recipe inspiration" packs provide premeasured amounts of multiple spices to make using them easier for the beginner cook (reason 3).

And, here's an example for Gen Z single men with research support.

To Men (gender) 18-23 (age range), who want to eat healthier (plus one) but don't cook (consumer insight), McCormick spices (brand) are the perfect solution (key message), because herbs and spices are healthy (reason 1), taste good (reason 2) and are easy to use since you can sprinkle them on your takeout and frozen foods (reason 3)

<u>Rationale/Support</u>

- As of 2018, there are 15.7 million Men 18-24 in the U.S. representing 9.7% of the total population. (2018)

- 67% of Gen Z care about the nutritional content of their food.(Valdez, 2018)

- Gen Z food delivery orders totaled $552 million in 2018. (Shoup, 2019)

- Gen Z is 23% more likely to eat frozen tv dinners, and 26% more likely to eat frozen breakfast entrees/sandwiches. They also are 29% more likely to eat shelf-to-microwave dinners, and are 10% more likely to eat dry packaged dinners, dinner mixes, and kits. (Granderson, 2019)
- Spices and herbs are healthy. They possess antioxidant, anti-inflammatory, antitumorigenic,

anticarcinogenic, and glucose- and cholesterol-lowering benefits as well as properties that positively affect cognition and mood.

It is also evident that frequent consumption of spicy foods is linked to a lower risk of death from cancer and ischemic heart and respiratory system diseases. (Jiang, 2019)

- Spices give aroma, color, flavor, and sometimes texture to food. (2020)

2018 American Community Survey. *census.gov.* Retrieved May 13, 2020, from https://data.census.gov/cedsci/all?t=Age%20and%20Sex&tid=ACSST1Y2018.S0101&hidePreview=false

Valdez, K. (2018, January) Why Now is the Time for Restaurants to Court Gen Z. *qsrmagazine.com.* Retrieved May 11, 2020, from https://www.qsrmagazine.com/outside-insights/why-now-time-restaurants-court-gen-z

Shoup, M. (2019, February 25) Gen Z will have a 'seismic' impact on the food industry, prioritizing convenience and functionality, says NPD group. *foodnavigator.com.* Retrieved May 8, 2020, from https://www.foodnavigator-usa.com/Article/2019/02/25/Gen-Z-will-have-seismic-impact-on-the-food-industry-prioritizing-convenience-and-functionality-says-NPD-Group?utm_source=copyright&utm_medium=OnSite&utm_campaign=copyright

Granderson, D. (2019, February 11) Gen Z Adults Seek Foods Fitting Their Busy, Yet Health Conscious Lifestyles. *prnewswire.com* Retrieved May 8, 2020, from https://www.prnewswire.com/news-releases/gen-z-adults-seek-foods-fitting-their-busy-yet-health-conscious-lifestyles-300793417.html

Jiang, T. (2019, March 1) Health Benefits of Culinary Herbs and Spices. *nih.gov.* Retrieved March 10, 2020, from https://www.ncbi.nlm.nih.gov/pubmed/30651162

(2020) Flavor Characteristics of Spices. *spicesinc.com.* Retrieved June 29, 2020, from https://www.spicesinc.com/p-3743-flavor-characteristics-of-spices.aspx

As you can see, while the brand - McCormick Spices - is the same for the last two positioning statements, the propositions are very different because the target has changed.

Part 3
How you say it (delivery)

Chapter 10. Memory

Speak first. Repeat at least three times.

We are hard-wired to believe that what we hear and read is true because initially all of our beliefs were formed through direct experiences. We saw, heard, and touched things with our own eyes, ears, and hands, so there was no question about whether or not the experience was true or false.

Unfortunately, this puts us in a poor position to understand and evaluate indirect experiences. And since our brains have been wired to favor efficiency over accuracy via the use of decision-making short-cuts, we tend to believe the first thing we hear. This is particularly true if what we hear conforms with our existing beliefs.[1]

Serial Position Effect

In 1885, German psychologist Hermann Ebbinghaus published his pioneering studies of memory. These include the discovery of the "serial position effect," which observed that words at the beginning and end of a list were more easily recalled than those in the middle.

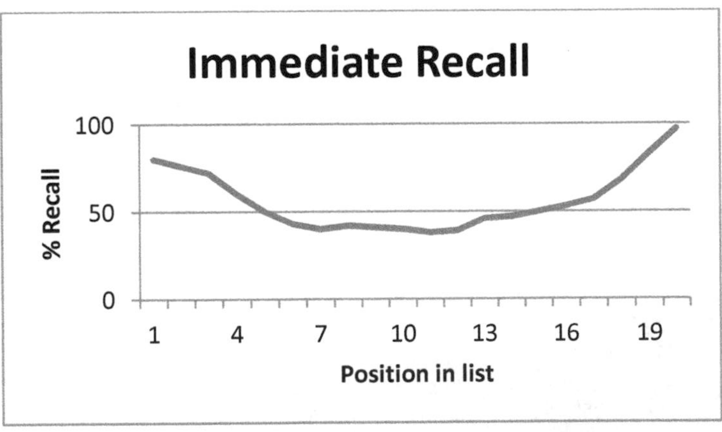

He postulated that the words at the beginning of the list were more easily recalled because they had more time to be committed to long-term memory. This is known as the "Primacy Effect." Words at the end of the list were more readily recalled because they were still in short term memory. This is known as the "Recency Effect."[2]

So not only are we more likely to believe the first thing that we hear, we are also more likely to remember it.

Carl Hovland's research on the order of presentation determined that the primacy effect was a more significant factor in influencing opinions for subjects with relatively weak desires for understanding. Those would of course be the "S" personality types.[3]

Effective frequency

Ebbinghaus also developed the forgetting curve, which established the fact that in the absence of reminders, after 31 days memory retention drops to 21%.

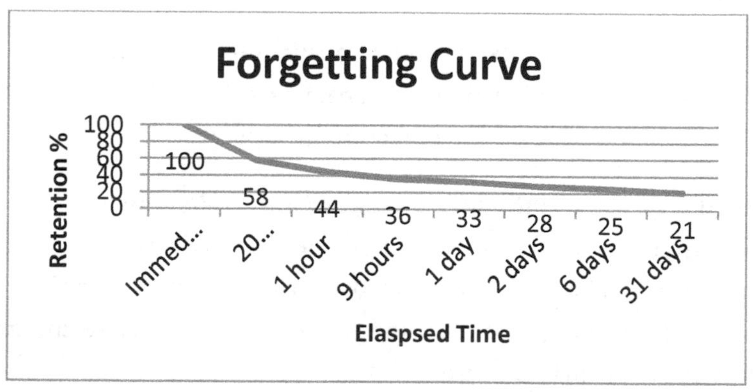

But, he also discovered the spacing effect, which showed that periodic reminders can have a significant positive effect on learning and retention.

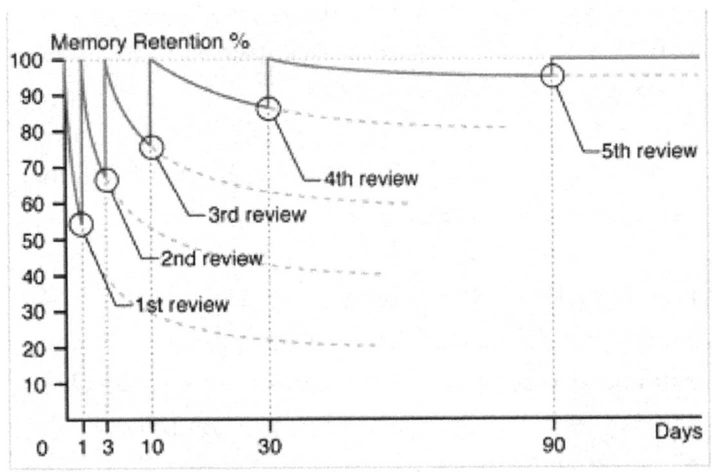

Note that in the model, after the third repetition retention is approximately 75%.[4]

This led marketers to develop the rule of threes - typically articulated as - "a person needs to see an ad three times before he remembers it." Thus, the minimum effective frequency for messaging was set at three.[5]

The reason why we need three exposures to a message is because we remember things in groups of three. That's why our phone numbers are arranged in groups of three.[6]

As to why three is the magic number, researchers believe it is because it is a sufficient set size for people to draw inferences. This was borne out by a study which found that people could judge the meaning of a new word after seeing it used in three different examples.[7]

And the Supreme Court found that three strikes laws were constitutional because we could infer from three felony convictions that the individual was a career criminal.

Of course other theories about effective frequency abound. Thomas Smith, a contemporary of Ebbinghaus, postulated that 20 exposures were necessary to make a sale.[8] Dr. Jeffrey Lant's "Rule of Seven," based on his experiments from the 60's and 70's, says you need seven points of contact to make a sale.[9]

This may be where the idea of message wear-out after eight exposures came from. But the world was a very different place then - no cable tv, no internet, no social media.

So, while eight exposures and out may have been the rule of thumb for marketers in the past, there is considerable evidence now that there is no such thing as message wear-out. This makes sense based on Krugman's data showing that when dealing with low involvement audiences (S's) we see gradual shifts in perception which are aided by message repetition. Therefore, more repetition equals more persuasion.[10]

A UK study of mobile advertising frequency determined that the sweet spot was 15-25 exposures. But for low consideration categories it may need to go up to 20-30.[11]

And a study on tv ads done by Millward Brown showed that awareness over time only changed in 6% of cases and that the change was just as likely to have gone in either direction. While ad effectiveness did not change at all.[12]

Illusory Truth effect

Research has also established that the more often we hear something the more likely it is that we will believe it is true. Repeated statements are easier to process. And we mistake familiarity for truth. Interestingly, this happens even if stored knowledge could have been used to detect a contradiction.

The rule of threes still applies, so we find that after a third exposure to a false statement, people are just as likely to believe that statement as they are a true statement they have heard only once. And several studies have shown that under some circumstances people will even believe assertions that are explicitly labeled as false.[13]

Cognitive Dissonance

Whether or not we even hear a message depends in part on whether or not it agrees with our views. A statement that supports the beliefs that we already hold is more easily processed and connected to previously held information in our brain, making it more memorable as well.

But when the statement conflicts with what we believe to be true we feel uncomfortable, because we have a need for harmony in our beliefs. This feeling of discomfort is called "cognitive dissonance" and we need to resolve it in order to feel at ease. Typically we do this by ignoring the new data - i.e. denial.

When my mother, a life-long smoker, found out that she was dying of lung cancer, she said: "I don't think it was the cigarettes that gave me cancer." She had two university degrees and knew the truth, but couldn't accept the result of her choices.

Another reaction to cognitive dissonance is to re-interpret the evidence so that it conforms to the original belief. So if the world didn't end on 1/1/2000 it's because man redeemed himself in the eyes of god.[14]

This is why it is so difficult to convince someone to change their mind once they believe something to be true. Humans are stubborn. And facts don't convince them to change their minds.

Chapter 11. Execution

Tell stories, words matter, visuals are most memorable.

Unlike effective frequency, a 2014 study confirmed that the optimal number of claims in a persuasive argument is three and that in fact an argument loses credibility if additional claims are added. In this instance, more is not better. Once enough information is received to draw an inference, any additional information given is perceived with skepticism.[1]

Research has also indicated that two-sided messages are more effective at changing opinions and maintaining opinion change. And they are also more resistant to counter propaganda.[2]

Storytelling

People learn by listening to stories. That's why we dream. The new information that we have learned that day is strung together with things we already know in a story format, which helps us to create the links necessary to put the new information into long term memory.[3]

Stories allow a person to feel and see the information, adding emotion to the basic facts, which is necessary to create a long-term memory. Stories help us make sense of abstract and complex subjects. They provide contextual links to knowledge we already have to help us connect the dots.[4]

Not surprisingly, research has shown that telling a story about a brand is more engaging and memorable than reciting a list of facts about it. And, it's also more compelling -- purchase intent for a story based ad, was 42% versus the norm of 33%.[5]

Storytelling in marketing has become increasingly popular due in part no doubt to the results of this research, but also because of the move away from buying things toward buying experiences instead. In an article about Millennials and wine, one admitted that he might have been more interested in a particular wine had the story about it been better.[6]

Words matter

We have seen that repetition causes belief in false statements. So does the use of negative emotional language, as one often sees in fake news. A 2017 study found that for each additional word, like "hate," "destroy," or "blame" the chance that a message will spread increases by about 20%. It's another example of "bad is stronger than good."

Although one does wonder whether some of the sharing of fake news is actually driven by the fact that it "seems off." But since any sharing is amplified by online algorithms that favor "popularity" as a measure of worthiness, fake news has exploded. Is it any wonder that a 2018 study showed that fake news stories were 70% more likely to be retweeted than real ones?[7]

When Diet Coke was first introduced, its name was a real turn-off for men. Remember, Men don't diet, they get in shape. So the company introduced Coke Zero just for them, in a macho black can. The Brits nicknamed it "Bloke Coke."[8] Dr. Pepper had similar success with Dr. Pepper Ten, which was launched with a $10 million "just for men" campaign.[9]

Reviews of help wanted postings revealed that use of the words "Rock Star" encourages more male applicants than female. Saying that a job requires a "passion for learning" attracts more women than men. And, if you use jargon such as "synergy" or "push the envelope" fewer non-whites will respond.[10]

Given the strength that a single word can have, is it any surprise that the U.S. government has strict rules about the use of the word "new?" Because new is such a strong word when it comes to motivating purchase, the law says it can only be used for six months after a brand introduction or reformation.

Framing

Research shows that even changing a single descriptive word can distort perceptions. In the classic psychology study by Loftus and Palmer (1974) *Reconstruction of Automobile Destruction*, participants to a car crash were asked how fast the cars were going when they crashed. Answers varied depending upon which verb questioners used to describe the event the participants had just witnessed. The harsher the word, the higher the speed estimate...[11]

Smashed = 40.8 mph
Collided = 39.3 mph
Bumped = 38.1 mph
Hit = 34 mph
Contacted = 31.8 mph

This is called framing. And how you frame an issue determines how it will be evaluated. That's why beef labeled 75% lean is more appealing than beef labeled 25% fat, even though they are the exact same thing.[12]

A letter to *New York Times* pointed out that framing DACA youth as "children of lawbreakers who entered the country illegally" evokes a different response from "young people who grew up believing in the American dream, lived responsible, respectable lives, and are willing to pay real money to obtain legal status." And even simply referring to Muslim-Americans as American-Muslims changes perceptions.

The Wall Street Journal has an interesting habit of using positive headlines followed by contradictory first sentences. For example, in a recent article the headline said: "America's Economy Is Healing Slowly." But the first line of text said: "The U.S. economy didn't deteriorate as badly in May as it did in April." And as the next line pointed out:" That's a far cry from saying that it is getting better." So where did that misleading headline come from?[13]

Clearly it is possible to reframe impressions and the same holds true for perceptions of a country. 20 years ago all anyone knew about Colombia was that the drug lords had taken it over. Then in 2008 the country rebranded itself with videos of its beaches, jungles, cities and mountains, and the tagline - "The risk is that you'll want to stay." It probably didn't hurt that "Narcos" was such a big hit on Netflix. The result? More than three million visitors in 2017, a 200% increase from 2006.[14]

But, perceptions that are anchored by a long held belief can be hard to change due to first impression bias. An example of this is the reluctance of people to pay even small amounts of money for apps. Why? Because over 90% of apps are free.[15]

Comparatives

Research shows that 12% of all thoughts are comparative. People compare themselves to benchmarks all the time. We compare ourselves to others. But we also compare our past decisions to future ones, seeking the optimal approach, consistency and loss avoidance.[16]

Comparatives are used frequently in communications. Comparing an unfamiliar product to a familiar one helps people understand its function. For instance, Zoom, which has taken off during the Covid-19 lockdown has been described as "Skype on steroids."

AT&T

Comparatives can also change perceptions by providing context. AT&T, a premium priced telecom service, once ran a campaign that characterized the price differential between it and its inferior competitors as being "just a few cents." This was visualized by showing a few coins in a hand at the end of a :15 second commercial.

It was an incredibly effective strategy. Because AT&T had deep pockets, the agency was able to track consumer perceptions of the brand weekly. When price perceptions began to rise, i.e. the perceived difference in cost between AT&T and its competitors, those commercials would air over the weekend, and like magic, the price perceptions would go back down the following week.

Comparatives are also used to connote superiority. Historically marketers shied away from direct comparisons with category leaders for fear that once the message was forgotten, only the name of the leading brand would be remembered. This is a valid concern.

Being vague when making comparisons also allows room for misleading claims. A Tide commercial that ran several years ago included this claim: "No other leading brand will make your whites whiter." Think about that. That's a parity claim. It doesn't say that Tide makes your whites the whitest they can be. It does say that a non-leading brand, probably bleach, can make your whites whiter. But what the brain hears is a superiority claim - "Tide makes your clothes whitest."

Naming names in direct comparisons is illegal in many countries. In the U.S. where it is allowed it has been periodically embraced. Some may remember the soda wars - Coke versus Pepsi - with its blind taste tests.

<u>Samsung vs. Apple</u>

More recently, Apple's stock rose to an all-time high in 2012 as anticipation built for the launch of the iPhone5. Then along came a satirical ad from Samsung for the Galaxy S3 which poked fun at the uncoolness of waiting on lines overnight for a phone with inferior features. The commercial was a huge viral hit with 120,000 shares on social media in less than 24 hours. Apple's stock price declined. The two companies continue to go at each other today, but not with the dramatic results realized previously.[17]

Visuals

Humans are visual creatures. And we have a remarkable ability to remember pictures. Research shows that people can remember more than 2,000 pictures with 90% accuracy for several days even with a short initial exposure. [18]

This far exceeds our ability to remember words. And in fact, neuroimaging experiments have shown that there is a qualitative difference in the ways that words and pictures are processed during memory formation.[19] Visuals trigger an emotional response, while words lead to more rational and linear thoughts.[20]

Adding photos or infographics to content increases readers' initial interest, emotional response and retention. When people hear information audibly, only 10 percent of said data is recalled three days later. Pair a pertinent image with the information, however, and 65 percent of it is retained after the same period.[21]

In one study, a story about a kidnapping which included visual materials caused more engagement and fear than one which did not. And left readers more likely to negotiate for the release of the captive.[22] It certainly makes one wonder if the U.S. would have stronger gun laws now if the photos of the children killed in the Sandy Hook Massacre had been released to the public.[23]

Research by PR Newswire showed that articles with images get 94% more views than those without. And BuzzSumo research found that articles with images inserted every 75-100 words were shared on social media twice as much as those without them.[24]

Color matters too. In particular, red. The color red has been shown to inhibit cognitive performance, increase dominance in competitive interactions and modulate mating behavior. In many situations it is associated with danger. So it shouldn't be surprising that use of the color red leads to more conservative choices and behavior.[25]

On the other hand, we are hard wired to relax when we see the color green. And the result is so strong that even a photo of nature on the wall can help us feel calmer.[26]

Because our visual memory is stronger than our verbal memory, we use a portion of our brain -- the Visual Word Form Area (VWFA) to convert words to pictures which we then store. This allows us to see a group of words as a visual comprised of the shapes that the letters make. The next time we see these words, we retrieve them as if they are a single visual, both faster and more accurately than we would if they were separate words.[27]

Logos, which combine a visual representation with words, can be particularly memorable. The most memorable ones, think Nike, Apple and McDonald's, were 13% more likely to get consumers' attention, 7% more likely to encourage consumers to learn more and 6% more likely to create an aura of uniqueness.

It's worth noting that since a recognizable logo stimulates trust, a change of logo can do just the opposite. Unless a good reason for the change is articulated, people will see it as a negative and assume that the product has changed for the worse.[28]

Typeface

There is a wealth of research available about typefaces, much of it conflicting. Serif type, which this book uses, is said to be more traditional and elegant, while sans-serif type such as Arial is considered more modern. Testing shows that serif type is slightly more legible. But that difference is attributed primarily to the fact that it allows for more white space around the letters. In fact, it is increased leading - i.e. the space between lines that results in the greatest improvements in comprehension.[29]

This is further supported by Rebecca Johnson's research which shows that double spacing after a sentence increases reading speed by 3%.[30]

Also of note were the results from a study of handwritten typefaces versus computer typefaces. Results show that handwritten typefaces create the perception of human presence, which leads to more favorable product evaluations and enhance the emotional attachment between consumers and products. An evaluation of the effect of handwritten typeface on purchase intent indicated that 30.4% of consumers made a purchase of products with handwritten typefaces versus 5.6% for machine typefaces.[31]

Packaging

Packaging is an integral part of the marketing process. The emergence of D2C products has led to an increased focus on packaging because it is one of the best branding tools available in a process that involves no face-to-face interaction. Part of the allure of subscription services that provide monthly items is the surprise of what people find when they open the box, so it makes sense that the box should enhance that experience.

Increasingly we are seeing examples of environmentally friendly/sustainable packaging - which serve to highlight the similar nature of the product or perhaps just the fact that the manufacturer understands that people are looking for easy ways to be green. Some startups are even delivering handsome presentations of reusable containers for first purchases followed by refills for follow-ups.[32]

They are all hoping that users will create unboxing videos and post them on their own social media to provide positive word-of-mouth.

<u>Tropicana</u>
Anyone who still doubts the importance of packaging needs only remember the Tropicana repackaging fiasco of 2009.

The company paid Arnell $35 million for a redesign, which led to a $33 million decline in sales (20%) in less than two months. At that point Tropicana decided to reverse course and return to the old packaging. Perhaps if the new packaging design didn't make every product in the line look the same, it might not have been so bad, but many consumers also felt that the new design screamed "generic." So they rejected it for that reason.[33]

On the opposite side of the coin is Coke's "Share a Coke" campaign featuring personalized bottles and cans. Launched in 2011, it reversed an eleven year sales decline. And, it is now a global seasonal event in 80 plus countries.[34]

Recent enhancements include family names on large bottles destined for family reunions, and college and NFL team names for football fans.[35]

Music

Music engages the areas of the brain involved in paying attention. Brain scans have shown a striking increase in activity in the right side of the brain when people listen to music. This side of the brain controls memory, reasoning, and problem-solving. All handy when making decisions.[36]

Research also shows that music is transmitted from generation to generation and shapes autobiographical memories as well as preferences and emotional responses. We call this "reminiscence bumps." And they are the reason why hearing a song from decades ago can transport us to another place and time.[37]

Initially commercials used custom jingles, written by soon to be known performers like Barry Manilow. Thanks to extreme repetition many of us can still recite some of those jingles today.

Once it became more acceptable for popular musicians to use their music for commercial purposes, we started hearing familiar tunes, sometimes even performed by the original artists. These songs have a distinct advantage in evoking the responses mentioned above.

Chevy

In the past few decades, original music has made a comeback. But this time the music is being written by artists who already have a following. And merchandising of the songs becomes part of the campaign, often through free downloads or premium CDs.

Chevy was the first company to have a major breakthrough with this idea, when John Mellencamp's "Our Country" was introduced as the new Chevrolet theme. It became so popular through this commercial that when it was released as a single, it shot to the top of the charts.[38]

Chapter 12. Creative Briefs

Focused briefs create better results.

The creative development process starts with the creative brief. The creative brief serves two primary purposes. The first is to get all the constituents overseeing creative strategy on the same page; the second is to inform the creative teams who will be handling creative development.

Teams typically consist of a copywriter who is an expert with words and an art director who is an expert on visuals. Due to the decentralized nature of marketing it is not uncommon for multiple teams working in different locations, on different pieces of the marketing mix, to use a single brief in order to maintain synergy.

But it can also make sense to do different briefs for different media, since a long-form medium like native advertising can incorporate much more information than a tweet can. And in some circumstances overall strategy might dictate the use of complementary messaging in different media, rather than identical messaging.

The creative brief is the strategic blueprint for the creative. It is a highly collaborative effort, and for most of the people involved in a marketing campaign, this is their best opportunity to positively impact the quality of the creative. Ideally the process begins with a client briefing and ends with client approval of a brief written by strategic planners.

The following creative brief format is based on those used at various advertising agencies. While other clients and agencies may use slightly different versions, this format contains all the information necessary to develop successful creative, and perhaps more importantly, does not contain room for ambiguity. Because, the most important factors in creating effective briefs are clarity and focus. And remember these days the people executing your briefs may not speak English as a first language.

The brief contains six elements that are critical for creative development. They are: target audience, consumer insight, key message, and three support points that provide reasons to believe the key message. The other elements in the brief provide the context for the project: objectives, geography, timing, tonality, etc. Together, all the pieces provide the direction necessary to develop creative.

In a perfect world, a creative brief would be one page. But, if back-up research is included, which it should be, it will be longer. The important part is to make sure that the key points in the brief do not contradict each other. Because, if they do, different constituents will have different expectations for the final creative product.

While it is tempting to use very broad messages, just as it is tempting to include everyone in your target audience, specifics sell. Unless they get bored exercising and are therefore seeking variety, people don't select a health club because it has lots of everything. They select a health club because it has the features they are looking for - maybe a 50 meter pool (Asphalt Green), yoga classes after work (Health & Racquet) or even a good place to mingle (Equinox).

If you have narrowed your audience correctly, it will be easy to focus your message on the one that will appeal most to them.

Let's walk through the format together.

Creative Brief (Creative Strategy Recommendation)

Campaign name
Date

Background
(What is the purpose of the project?)

Remember, the primary purpose of this document is to brief creative teams, so include only the information they will need to know to develop the creative. Err on the side of brevity. The briefing will be presented in person, so creatives will have an opportunity to ask questions if they are unclear about something. If the creative being developed is part of an integrated marketing campaign being developed by several teams this is the place to explain that, and how this piece fits with the rest.

Communications objectives
(What do we expect to accomplish? How do we intend to measure results?)

You must set an objective for a campaign in order to be able to measure its success. In the past the objectives often involved a communications measure such as increasing awareness. And measurement of achievement of that objective was done via pre and post polling. In some cases this is still being done today.

But increasingly, this somewhat soft objective has been replaced by hard sales quotas, e.g. increase sales by 15,000 units. And, in order to be perceived as effective, a campaign needs to result in a minimum of a 10% sales increase. If it does not meet this minimum threshold then it is unlikely that it will be repeated.

Creative elements

(What types of materials are being produced? tv, radio, etc.)

This is a list of the media to be used in the campaign so the creative team will understand what it needs to provide. Include lengths of the television spots (e.g., 30 seconds) and sizes and specs of print ads (e.g., full-page, 4-color), podcast lengths, and any other relevant information.

Typically, one format is used to present several ideas during the first creative presentation so constituents can pick a direction. Once a direction is agreed upon the additional creative elements are developed.

Geography

(Where is the product/service currently available?)

Since specifics sell it is important to know where a campaign is going to run. Global, national, local, etc. Based on that information an approach can be tailored the audience, as it was with the Manhattan Mini Storage campaign.

Timing

(When is the campaign scheduled to run?)

Here too there are opportunities for connecting. Most campaigns are seasonal. Many times it's because marketers can't afford a year-long presence. But it's also because most brands are not bought at equal levels throughout the year.

Holiday marketing is of course the biggest -- especially Christmas/Chanukah/New Year's. But "back to school" can also be part of an effective strategy. For some people, the new year begins in September -- health club attendance rises, closets are cleaned out and new cars are bought.[1]

Target

(Who are we trying to reach? age, income, marital status, etc.)

As discussed previously, a target definition should include at a minimum -- gender, age range, and a plus one (additional descriptor).

Consumer insight

(What do we know about the way our target thinks or feels that can be used to create an emotional connection with them?)

It bears repeating - all decisions are emotional. The role of the consumer insight is to facilitate an emotional connection with the target. It is the place where the psychology. sociology, and anthropology that we discussed in previous chapters is incorporated into the creative development process.

It must be singular. It's hard enough to evoke one emotion in a campaign, trying to communicate more than one will be confusing and is likely to be unsuccessful.

Key message

(What is the single thought we intend to communicate?)

Key messages need to as focused and clear as possible. Multiple thoughts don't work because they become confusing. The key message should be the natural response to the consumer insight. So if your insight is that men are worried about losing their hair and your product addresses that issue, your key message would be - Product X cures baldness.

Typically briefs are written so that the consumer insight provides the audience connection while the key message and support points focus on brand features.

Mastercard

Consider the award winning Mastercard "Priceless" campaign - still going strong after decades. The introductory commercial included a dad and his son bonding over baseball. (According to Jeroen Bours, CEO of Darling Advertising & Design, who created the campaign with his partner Joyce King Thomas - it was a Mets game!)

And while the structure of the campaign may be the thing that is most remembered and parodied -

- Two tickets: $46.
- Two hotdogs, two popcorns, two sodas: $ 27.
- One autographed baseball: $50.
- Real conversation with 11-year-old son; Priceless.
- There are some things money can't buy. For everything else, there's Mastercard.

think about what the key message of this commercial says - "Money can buy happiness." Oh wait that's actually "Credit can buy happiness." Now that's a promise that overextended Americans can really relate to, and who doesn't want to bond with their children?

But functional key messages may not be the best approach given that we are trying to stir emotions. During testing for the launch of Uncle Ben's Country Rice Dishes, an emotional key message option - "based on recipes from country inns" far outperformed the two functional alternatives - "rice and vegetable combinations" and "all in one meal." As a result the product line was renamed.

<u>Support</u>

(What are the three reasons to believe the key message?)

Often key messages end up being fairly broad - e.g. this is the best shampoo ever. That's why we need support points to complete the proposition and provide reasons to believe it. And as we have seen three is the magic number if we want to persuade.

Start with your strongest point, in case the brief is used for short-form media that will only accommodate one support point. Remember that being specific increases believability and relatability.

<u>Fusion Razor</u>
Here's an example of a very straightforward brief used by Gillette to launch the Fusion razor -

Key message: The best razor ever

Support:
1. It's new from Gillette - the razor category leader
2. It has five blades on one side of the razor for a loser shave
3. It has a single precision blade on the other side for better trimming

The support points are what makes this argument persuasive. Note how specific they are. And that the first one uses both authority (Gillette) and social proof (category leader).

It was a winning strategy - the fusion razor captured 55% of all new razor sales in the U.S. just four weeks after its launch.[2]

<u>Tonality</u>
(Is the ad introductory? What type of mood are we trying to achieve?)

If this is a new product, it should be addressed in the creative. It's also important to indicate if the creative should take a fun approach, scientific approach, etc. as this will impact executional choices during creative development.

Mandatories

(What are the executional elements that must be included?)

These are things that must be included in the ad, such as toll-free phone numbers, and Web site addresses, logos, etc. Try to keep them to a minimum. There really is no reason to include a URL unless it is specifically dedicated for the effort, because most people will just google the company name to get to the website.

Chapter 13.
Creative Strategy Recommendation

Here is a repeat of the McCormick Spices positioning statement for single Gen Z men from chapter nine.

To Men (gender) 18-24 (age range), who want to eat healthier (plus one) but don't cook (consumer insight), McCormick spices (brand) are the perfect solution (key message), because herbs and spices are healthy (reason 1), taste good (reason 2) and are easy to use since you can sprinkle them on your takeout and frozen foods (reason 3)

As you can see it defines the proposition, but is not specific enough to make a compelling brief. Here's an example of a creative brief for a campaign that would fit under the umbrella positioning that it provides.

McCormick Spices Creative Strategy Recommendation

Campaign Name: Sprinkle Some McCormick On It

Date: 1/20

Background

(What is the purpose of the project? What are the defined parameters?)

McCormick Spices currently focuses its primary marketing efforts on Women 25-54 with children under 18. We see an opportunity to reach out to Men 18-24 who want to eat healthier, but don't cook, since spices can be sprinkled on takeout and frozen foods, making them both tastier and healthier.

Communications Objectives

(What do we expect to accomplish? How do we intend to measure results?)

For the effort to pay out we will need to see a 10% increase in sales by the end of December.

Creative Elements

(What types of materials are being produced? tv? radio? etc.)

- :15 & :30 second video
- Bar collateral
- Game signage

Geography

(Where is service currently available? Where will it expand within the next 12 months?)

This is a U.S. national campaign.

Timing

(When is the campaign scheduled to run?)

The campaign will run from August 2021 through December 2021. If objectives are met, it will be continued through May 2022.

Target

(Who are we trying to reach? age, income, marital status, etc.)

Men 18-23 who want to eat healthier.

As of 2018, there are 15.7 million Men 18-24 in the U.S. representing 9.7% of the total population. (2018) It is estimated that globally Gen Z has over $140 billion in buying power. (Davis, 2020) In the U.S., they spent $78 billion in restaurants in 2016. (Valdez, 2018) 42% of Men 18-24 do not live with their parents, 29% of them are married. (2017)

67% of Gen Z care about the nutritional content of their food. (Valdez, 2018) They are more likely to look for organic or natural foods, and prefer foods without artificial ingredients. They are also more likely to be vegetarians (7%). (Granderson, 2019)

Almost half (41%) say they would pay more for foods they perceive as healthier (2020) And, in the past year, 28% of 18-24 year-olds tried the Paleo diet, 26% went gluten-free, and 24% tried whole 30. (Sloan, 2019)

Spices and herbs are healthy. They possess antioxidant, anti-inflammatory, antitumorigenic, anticarcinogenic, and glucose- and cholesterol-lowering benefits as well as properties that positively affect cognition and mood. Frequent consumption of spicy foods is linked to a lower risk of death from cancer and ischemic heart and respiratory system diseases. (Jiang, 2019)

Gen Z is the most ethnically diverse generation -- 48% are non-white. (Fry & Parker, 2018) Perhaps that is part of the reason why 79% of Gen Z eats "specialty foods" and 42% say they favor "street food." (Newhart, 2019) Clearly they are open to experimenting with new flavors and cuisines.

Consumer Insight

(What do we know about the way our target thinks or feels that can be used to make an emotional connection with them?)

They don't cook. They takeout, order in and defrost.

In 2018, Gen Z ate more than 40% of lunches and dinners out. (Sloan, 2019) In total, they made 14.6 billion restaurant visits -- one quarter of all restaurant visits. (McSweeney, 2019) But, this still represents a 26% decline in interest in eating out at full service restaurants. (Noyes, 2017)

They simply have better things to do with their time than sit in a restaurant. So what do they do? They order takeout. Gen Z, ages 8-23, orders more takeout than any other generation - 24% do it 3 - 4 times in a typical week. (Sweeney, 2018)

Gen Z food delivery orders totaled $552 million in 2018. Even though they are currently ages 8-23, which means a large portion of the generation is too young to participate. (Shoup, 2019)

74% of Gen Z eats snacks between meals. And 23% say they prefer to build a meal of appetizers.

They are also 23% more likely to eat frozen tv dinners, and 26% more likely to eat frozen breakfast entrees/sandwiches. They also are 29% more likely to eat shelf-to-microwave dinners, and are 10% more likely to eat dry packaged dinners, dinner mixes, and kits. (Granderson, 2019)

Key Message

(What is the single thought we intend to communicate?)

Adding McCormick Spices will make what you eat and drink healthier.

Support

(What are the reasons to believe the key message?)

1. Cinnamon lowers blood sugar and cholesterol. And you can sprinkle it in your coffee. (Rao & Gan, 2014)

2. Garlic can prevent and treat heart attacks (Bayan, Koulivand & Gorji, 2014) oregano has anti-viral properties which may be helpful in a Covid-19 world, (Leyva-Lopez, Gutierrez-Grijalva, Vazquez-Olivo & Heredia, 2017) and hot red chili peppers can reduce mortality by 13%. (Chopan & Littenberg, 2017) They also all make takeout pizza taste better.

3. And for the 46% of Gen Z who say chicken is their first choice protein, (McSweeney, 2019) there's rosemary. It contains antioxidants that can help prevent aging and might prevent Alzheimer's disease. (Habtemariam, 2016)

Tonality

(Is the ad introductory? Is it focused on acquisition or retention, etc?)

This may be the first time the target is learning about McCormick and the health benefits of herbs and spices.

Mandatories

(What are the executional elements that must be included?)

McCormick logo and tagline

Next Steps

Pending agreement to the creative brief, we will begin creative development.

2018 American Community Survey. *census.gov.* Retrieved May 13, 2020, from https://data.census.gov/cedsci/all?t=Age%20and%20Sex&tid=ACSST1Y2018.S0101&hidePreview=false

Davis, D. (2020, January 28) Gen Zers have a spending power of over $140 billion, and it's driving the frenzy of retailers and brands trying to win their dollars. *businessinsider.com.* Retrieved May 13, 2020, from https://www.businessinsider.com/retail-courts-gen-z-spending-power-over-140-billion-2020-1

Valdez, K. (2018, January) Why Now is the Time for Restaurants to Court Gen Z. *qsrmagazine.com.* Retrieved May 11, 2020, from https://www.qsrmagazine.com/outside-insights/why-now-time-restaurants-court-gen-z

(2017. December 4) The Majority of 18-24-Year-Olds Live in Their Parents' Home, As Do 1 in 6 Older Millennials. *marketingcharts.com.* Retrieved May 13, 2020, from https://www.marketingcharts.com/demographics-and-audiences-81471

Valdez, K. (2018, January) Why Now is the Time for Restaurants to Court Gen Z. *qsrmagazine.com.* Retrieved May 11, 2020, from https://www.qsrmagazine.com/outside-insights/why-now-time-restaurants-court-gen-z

Granderson, D. (2019, February 11) Gen Z Adults Seek Foods Fitting Their Busy, Yet Health Conscious Lifestyles. *prnewswire.com* Retrieved

May 8, 2020, from https://www.prnewswire.com/news-releases/gen-z-adults-seek-foods-fitting-their-busy-yet-health-conscious-lifestyles-300793417.html

(2020, April 24) How Restaurants Can Please the Members of Generation Z. *aaronallen.com* Retrieved May 8, 2020, from https://aaronallen.com/blog/gen-z-food-trends

Sloan, A. (2019, July 1) Demographic Disrupters. *ift.org.* Retrieved May 8, 2020, from https://www.ift.org/news-and-publications/food-technology-magazine/issues/2019/july/features/food-purchasing-and-consumption-generalization-preferences

Fry, R. & Parker, K. (2018, November 15) Early Benchmarks Show 'Post-Millennials' on Track to Be Most Diverse, Best-Educated Generation Yet. *pewresearch.org.* Retrieved May 11, 2020, from https://www.pewsocialtrends.org/2018/11/15/early-benchmarks-show-post-millennials-on-track-to-be-most-diverse-best-educated-generation-yet/

Jiang, T. (2019, March 1) Health Benefits of Culinary Herbs and Spices. *nih.gov.* Retrieved March 10, 2020, from https://www.ncbi.nlm.nih.gov/pubmed/30651162

Newhart, B. (2019, January 22) Shopping small: 79% of Gen Z buys specialty foods. *beveragedaily.com.* Retrieved May 11, 2020, from https://www.beveragedaily.com/Article/2019/01/22/Shopping-small-79-of-Gen-Z-buys-specialty-foods

Sloan, A. (2019, July 1) Demographic Disrupters. *ift.org.* Retrieved May 8, 2020, from https://www.ift.org/news-and-publications/food-technology-magazine/issues/2019/july/features/food-purchasing-and-consumption-generalization-preferences

McSweeney, R. (2019, November 18) Generation Z Food Trends and Eating Habits. *upserve.com.* Retrieved May 8, 2020, from https://upserve.com/restaurant-insider/generation-z-new-food-trends/

Noyes, J. (2017, June) Surefire Tips to Bring Gen Z Into Your Restaurant. *qsrmagazine.com.* Retrieved May 8, 2020, from https://www.qsrmagazine.com/outside-insights/surefire-tips-bring-gen-z-your-restaurant

Sweeney, E. (2018, July 9) Gen Z Just Wants To Watch Netflix And Get Takeout, And It's Affecting Restaurants. *huffpost.com.* Retrieved May 8, 2020, from https://www.huffpost.com/entry/gen-z-restaurants-takeout_n_5b33a30de4b0b5e692f35f13

Shoup, M. (2019, February 25) Gen Z will have a 'seismic' impact on the food industry, prioritizing convenience and functionality, says NPD group. *foodnavigator.com.* Retrieved May 8, 2020, from https://www.foodnavigator-usa.com/Article/2019/02/25/Gen-Z-will-have-seismic-impact-on-the-food-industry-prioritizing-convenience-and-functionality-says-NPD-Group?utm_source=copyright&utm_medium=OnSite&utm_campaign=copyright

Granderson, D. (2019, February 11) Gen Z Adults Seek Foods Fitting Their Busy, Yet Health Conscious Lifestyles. *prnewswire.com* Retrieved May 8, 2020, from https://www.prnewswire.com/news-releases/gen-z-adults-seek-foods-fitting-their-busy-yet-health-conscious-lifestyles-300793417.html

Rao, P. & Gan, S. (2014, April 10) Cinnamon: A Multifaceted Medicinal Plant. *nih.gov.* Retrieved May 11, 2020, from https://www.ncbi.nlm.nih.gov/pmc/articles/PMC4003790/

Bayan, L., Koulivand, P., & Gorji, A. (2014, January) Garlic: a review of potential therapeutic effects. *Avicenna Journal of Phytomedicine.* Retrieved May 11, 2020, from https://www.ncbi.nlm.nih.gov/pmc/articles/PMC4103721/

Leyva-Lopez, N., Gutierrez-Grijalva, E., Vazquez-Olivo, G. & Heredia, J. (2017, June 6) Essential Oils of Oregano: Biological Activity beyond Their Antimicrobial Properties. *Molecules* Retrieved May 11, 2020, from https://www.ncbi.nlm.nih.gov/pmc/articles/PMC6152729/

Chopan, M. & Littenberg, B. (2017, January 9) The Association of Hot Red Chili Pepper Consumption and Mortality: A Large Population-Based

Cohort Study. *PLoS ONE.* Retrieved May 11, 2020, from https://www.ncbi.nlm.nih.gov/pmc/articles/PMC5222470/

McSweeney, R. (2019, November 18) Generation Z Food Trends and Eating Habits. *upserve.com.* Retrieved May 8, 2020, from https://upserve.com/restaurant-insider/generation-z-new-food-trends/

Habtemariam, S. (2016, January 28) The Therapeutic Potential of Rosemary (*Rosmarinus officinalis*) Diterpenes for Alzheimer's Disease. *Evidence-based Complementary and Alternative Medicine.* Retrieved May 11, 2020, from *https://www.ncbi.nlm.nih.gov/pmc/articles/PMC4749867/*

Part 4
Where you say it (media)

Chapter 14. Media Planning

Maximize efficiency, minimize waste.

The goal of media planning is to reach as many people in the target group as you can, as efficiently as possible. As noted in Chapter 2, marketers are now focusing more on smaller well defined targets because doing so enables them to create more effective messaging. The same is true for media planning.

Media costs are based on the size of the audience they attract. Buy fewer eyeballs and it will cost you less money. That's why media planning is the art of balancing audience composition (higher percentage of the target) and coverage (higher numbers of the target) when making selections. Targeted media provides a greater proportion of prospects. Mass media provides more prospects, but they will be mixed in with people who aren't prospects.

Delivering messages to anyone who isn't part of the designated target is unlikely to yield a sale and therefore is considered "waste." The first priority in media planning is to select properties with high levels of target composition. This maximizes efficiency because you are reaching more of the people you want to reach and fewer of the people you don't want to reach.

The explosion of media in the past few decades has led to the creation of many more targeted media opportunities both online and off. For instance, HGTV by definition delivers people who are interested in their homes and by extension home improvements. While it is true that those individuals can also be found consuming other media, it is unlikely that they will be represented in such high concentrations in those media as they are on HGTV. Therefore HGTV represents the most efficient way to reach the target.

It is only after highly targeted opportunities are fully optimized that a marketer will consider other media to extend reach and increase coverage.

The other key component to keep in mind when developing media plans is the fact that integrated marketing campaigns, i.e. those that include more than one medium, are more effective. Typically, when an individual is a light user of one medium, he is a heavy user of a different one. So, intuitively it makes sense to use multiple types of media to reach a broader range of people. Research supports this hypothesis.

It also suggests that multi-media campaigns are more effective at achieving conversion.[1] In the digital age they are certainly responsible for amplifying messaging.

Old Spice

"The Man Your Man Could Smell Like" campaign from Old Spice was based on the consumer insight that many men just use whatever toiletries they find in the bathroom. Therefore while the final user was a man, the purchaser was a woman.

The television commercial featuring Isaiah Mustafa was an immediate hit. It's impact was multiplied by 186 highly personalized response videos that were released on YouTube. In a single week views of the personalized ads surpassed the nearly 29 million videos of the four television ads. By the end of the first month they had more than 34 million aggregate views and a billion PR impressions as they drove a borage of news coverage and parodies. And, Old Spice's Facebook fan interaction grew by 800%.

The effort stimulated growth of social media followers - 80,000 on Twitter, and 630,000 on Facebook, bumped traffic to OldSpice.com by 300%. An inspired fan created a website where people could download voicemail messages that sounded like Mr. Mustafa and many memes were shared.[2]

Actual media selection should be done based on research. With the abundance of data now available the trick is to make sure that you are interpreting it correctly.

For instance, Facebook is the mass medium of social media. As of May 2020, they have 2.45 billion monthly users. These include people from all generations. And given how many there are on the platform you could easily make the case that you will find more Gen Z on Facebook than on any other social network. However it is not the platform of their choice.

A deeper dive into Facebook statistics shows that the fastest growing demographic on the platform are users 65+. And that usage among teens 13-17 is down to 51% versus 71% in 2015. And while you can still reach teens on Facebook it is easier to reach them on their preferred platforms - Snapchat, YouTube and Instagram, since they interact with these platforms more often than they do with Facebook.[3] And you'll want to keep an eye on Tik Tok too.

In fact, generational preferences make a huge difference in media consumption. Boomers like television, QVC and direct mail, while Gen X favors YouTube. Millennials prefer live events and Instagram, while Gen Z favors Snapchat. Generation Alpha, our newest generation may prefer voice -

time will tell. But in the meantime refer to the most detailed up-to-date research you can find before making media selections.

Email

For the past decade, email has delivered the best return-on-investment for marketers. For every $1 spent, email marketing generates $38 in ROI.[4]

According to McKinsey & Company research, email marketing is up to 40 times more effective than social media. The rate at which emails prompt purchases is three times higher than social media and the average order value is 17% higher.[5]

Emails with personalized subject lines are 26% more likely to be opened. And, customized landing pages (those that go directly to the item) increase conversion rates by more than 25%. Marketers have achieved a 760% increase in email revenue from segmented campaigns. And A/B testing improves conversion by 49%.[6]

But don't forget that at least 50% of emails were opened on mobile in 2018, and presumably it's higher in 2020. Only 8% of them click the link though. Many open the email a second time from their computer, and are then 65% more likely to click through. Not surprisingly it varies with age. 40% of people 18 years old and under will always open an email on mobile first. Only 8% of those between 56 and 67 do.[7]

Another important thing to keep in mind is email frequency. While some data say there is no such thing as too much frequency, the number one reason that people unsubscribe from emails is too much frequency. And 45.8% cite it as the reason they flag the emails as spam.[8]

The sweet spot for open rates may be four to eight emails a month. But the sales to click rate improves at fewer than four.[9]

Social Media

As social media has matured we are seeing preference patterns for various targets. Pinterest appeals to older, better educated women. LinkedIn appeals to professionals, making it the best platform for B2B marketers. Instagram and Snapchat are teen favorites, while Reddit attracts young men. Twitter skews toward young Asian men. Why? The relationship between the platform and the NBA may explain their preference.[10]

And while the aggregate numbers for social media are huge - particularly for Facebook, specific feeds are delivering far fewer viewers.[11]

For example, in a head to head comparison for a Thursday Night football game, Twitter NFL delivered 327,000 viewers in an average minute versus 17.5 million for CBS. That's why digital properties tend to cite cumulative audience numbers instead of average minute.[12]

Facebook sells specific demos. Restaurant chains can run campaigns targeting spicy food lovers, while moving companies can find users who are "very likely" to relocate soon. And it seems very likely that the Russian Facebook ads designed to suppress the Black American vote in 2016, were successful.[13]

Although perhaps not as successful as those run on Instagram where 70% of users are under 35; And 43% of Black Americans are platform users.[14]

But, feedback on Facebook has actually been mixed. Perhaps social media is better at selling ideas than it is products.

Consumer packaged goods manufacturer P&G indicated that they were having less success with targeted demos on Facebook than they were with broader definitions. So they have switched to buying the latter.[15]

This has created an opportunity for smaller brands to buy targeted demos at lower rates. Arts Japan 2020 saw its cost per engagement decrease significantly after it started targeting audiences whose interests included at least five manifestations of Japanese culture such as woodblock prints, Ikebana or Kabuki.[16]

On the other hand, filmmaker Matthew Wilson found greater success targeting "people who watch movies on Amazon and are interested in comedies" than he did "people who liked the movie *Pretty Woman.*"[17]

Perhaps the difference is due to the fact that the first measures activity, while the second involves "likes" which are known to be of little value to marketers. In fact, a study showed that only 1% of users who like a brand on Facebook will actually visit the brand's Facebook page.[18]

Social media does seem to work particularly well for artists, as it allows them to connect directly with their fan bases.

The most savvy marketers are using multiple channels and assigning different roles to them. For instance, Rihanna posts glamour shots on Instagram and videos of "regular" Rihanna shopping for *Apple Jacks* on Snapchat. The Rock promotes his movies and shares personal stories on Facebook. One thing they have in common? Frequent content updates to keep people coming back for more. Kim Kardashian posts an average of two images a day on Instagram, and has since 2012.[19]

But it's worth remembering that search engines are 300% more effective than social media when it comes to driving traffic to a content website.[20] That having been said, more consumers are doing their searching directly on Facebook and Amazon, rather than Google. In fact, a 2018 study showed that 46.7% of US internet users start their product searches on Amazon.[21]

Visuals

Human preference for visuals includes digital, where infographics get shared three times as much as other forms of content on social media. Facebook posts with visuals get 37% more engagement. And tweets with visuals are retweeted 150% more than those without them.[22]

But perhaps more important is the use and growth of video. One only needs to visit Times Square NYC to see video billboards are more engaging than 2D. Presumably they are also more persuasive because video is better suited for storytelling and generating emotions among viewers.

As more video has been posted, people have begun to rely on it for decision-making. Research shows, that 50% of internet users looked for videos related to a product or service before visiting a store.[23]

80% of them say that it gives them more confidence when buying a product. Maybe because 50% say their biggest concern when shopping online is that the product won't look the same when it arrives. Product demos are most popular, with 69% saying they are the most helpful in making purchases. Also of aid are consumer testimonials (16%) and explainer videos (15%)[24]

Product reviews

88% of consumers trust online reviews as much as personal recommendations. 72% will take action only after reading a positive review. 86% of people will hesitate to buy from a business that has negative reviews online.[25]

That's a pretty interesting when Amazon's own studies show that roughly 30% of online reviews are inauthentic.[26]
But as with the hotel towel experiment, it appears that the simple act of using a product or service that an individual is considering buying pushes the "someone like me" button for the potential purchaser despite the fact that there is no reason to believe that this is actually true.

Out-of-Home

OOH is the oldest form of advertising. Egyptians employed tall stone obelisks to publicize laws and treaties and the Romans used wildposting, i.e. multiple posters, to promote candidates for Senate in 150 BC. Marketers have always valued outdoor for its ability to deliver mass audiences, and now that television is less able to do so, OOH is being used for a variety of broad reach efforts.

Moreover, research shows that OOH is the number one preferred format for Millennials and Gen Z. And that one out of every four consumers will post an image of an outdoor ad to Instagram.[27]

The primary issue marketers have with OOH is the long lead times it requires, typically six months at a minimum. Other issues include time-run commitments, which are generally for at least a month, and the inability to make creative changes during a run.

The move to digital is erasing all these concerns. Digital billboards can be developed more quickly, don't require

months for printing, can be targeted more precisely and changed frequently. They can even be interactive.
The ability to change copy based on time of day allows companies to tailor messages. For example, a fast food chain can run ads for breakfast sandwiches in the morning and burgers in the afternoon. And a billboard in Chicago's O'Hare airport ran creative that changes languages based on where the arriving flight originated.[28]

Interactive digital marketing can also include text messages and bar codes that viewers can access for more information, contests, and downloads, as well as plug-in boxes that allow people to use their headphones to sample songs and kiosks with touch screens.

Events

OOH also includes live events, another area of strong growth, no doubt aided by the move toward buying experiences rather than things. 98% of attendees say events increase purchase intent, while 65% of consumers purchase products or services during events.[29]

Events that are shared through both traditional and social media also have the added advantage of increasing reach. A fast food chain which sponsored a promotion at a live NBA basketball game saw an average increase in traffic of 8.4% within 24 hours of the game. BTW, the data used to support that statistic was supplied by cell phone companies.[30]

Voice

Voice is poised to become the next big thing. Podcasts are soaring, traditional radio is hanging in and Alexa is our new best friend.

Radio reaches 85% of all consumers every week. 65% of listening is done outside the home, and most listen in the car. But usage is also going up at home driven by people who have smart speakers.[31]

Stations are narrow casted to targeted segments who often have close ties to online talent. Maria Molito of Q104.3 has been with the station since 1996.[32] She is a well known dog lover, often attending pet adoption events with fans in tow. In May 2020 @anieves913 sent her a face mask with puppies on it. Maria posted a picture on Twitter at @mariamilito[33]

55% of Americans have listened to a podcast, 37% in the last month. Smartphones are driving growth. Heavy users listen away from home, most often at work.[34]

Meanwhile smart speaker ownership growth is explosive. In March 2020 it was estimated that 76 million American homes (27%) had smart speakers, and the mean number of speakers per home is 2.2.[35]

People not only use them to listen to music, they use them to turn on the lights. They also ask them questions.

Based on a recent study by Voicebot, questions about music are number one at 55%. But 36% ask questions about news,

35% about movies, 28% for how-to-instructions, 25% about products and 23% for restaurants.[36]

What the article didn't say was how many of those questions they asked were designed to let Alexa/Siri make decisions for them as opposed to just seeking information.

To avoid the angst of decision-making some people may be quite willing to cede what they consider unimportant choices - like toiletries - to another entity. And if they perceive that entity to be an expert source they would happily take the recommendation offered.

It seems that 85% of voice assistant users have purchased an item suggested by smart speakers despite the fact that it may have differed from their initial intent. And, 37% of voice purchasers 18-34 "always" or "often" purchase the first option selected for them by voice assistants.[37]

It's just so much easier to let someone else, or something else decide.

Television

After email, network television is the most effective form of marketing. That why even D-to-C brands, like Allbirds and Casper expanded into television when funding to do so became available. In fact a 2018 survey of 13 D-to-C brands showed a 42% increase in national television spending to $137 million. A further 34% increase was estimated for 2019, as well as a 25% increase in 2020, which is unlikely to happen. But the trend is clear.[38]

What did these newbies gain from their first television advertising efforts? An immediate lift in website visits ranging from 11% to 1075%.[39]

It's worth noting that part of the reason that at least one B2C company, Bombas, began spending money on television was a desire to reduce their dependency on Facebook. While Heidi Zak the co-founder of ThirdLove, indicated that her brand had reached the saturation point on social media and needed to expand to television to reach new prospects.[40] Composition first, then coverage.

How effective is television? One recent study found that television's lift was seven times better than paid search and five times better than online display ads.[41]

In a different study, search delivered the highest percentage of media-driven sales for the first two weeks of a campaign; 29% versus 23% for television and 10% for print. But in the six to 18 months following a campaign, TV delivers a 2.4 times increase in sales versus the amount generated in the first two weeks, while search drops to .8 times more and print to 1.2 times more.

Television also has the highest multiplier affect across other channels. It can boost the performance of cinema advertising by up to 56%; print, radio, online display and social media by 31%; and direct mail, online video, video-on-demand and outdoor by up to 22%.[42]

TV's success lies in the fact that it delivers large audiences. The largest reach program -- The Super Bowl, delivers over 100 million people. Network television average primetime audiences range from seven million to nine million. Cable channels audiences are lower with top performer ESPN delivering 1.8 million people. But since those viewers consist primarily of young men, a difficult target to reach elsewhere in television, it is an extremely efficient buy for many marketers.[43]

In cross platform campaigns, the average number of impressions from tv are nearly eight times greater than those for digital.[44] Therefore, it's not surprising that a Sr. VP for global advertising at American Express noted that they need to run digital for two weeks to get the same lift they do from one day of television.[45]

Global data echoes these findings. In Australia, an average tv campaign achieves a $1.70 in return for every dollar invested. In Belgium, tv generates 42% recall versus 15% for YouTube. On France, traffic to an advertisers website increases by 44% during a tv campaign. And in the UK adding tv to a campaign results in a 40% increase in effectiveness.[46]

People of all ages still watch lots of tv. According to a recent Nielsen report people 18+ watch an average of five hours of television per day, while spending only 19 minutes per day on multimedia devices. And the average Millennial spends more time watching tv than eating, drinking, shopping and watching YouTube combined.[47]

That having been said, television has been increasingly skewing toward older, less affluent Americans. The median age for live tv viewers in 2018 was 56, versus 38 for total U.S.[48] And, based on the latest American time use data from the census, unemployed people watch almost twice as much tv as employed people, and lower weekly earners watch 50% more tv than their more affluent counterparts.[49]

Once the best information available about television audiences was broad strokes demographic data like "Women 18-24." But now that Nielsen can merge shopper loyalty-card data with their tv viewership data much more specific information is available. For instance we know that high-income business travelers watch *Freaks of Nature*, while Hispanic bacon lovers prefer *It's Me or The Dog.*[50]

The Weather Channel has determined that beer sales go up in Chicago during the summer after three consecutive days of below-average temperatures. While sunnier warmer summer days in New York lead to more sales of healthy snacks. Taking advantage of this granular data, Pantene shampoo bought a schedule of "humid days" and extended the effort into mobile to encourage spontaneous purchases on bad hair days.[51]

This data also allows marketers to identify less expensive programs that deliver higher audience composition, an opportunity Obama's campaign took full advantage of in 2012 by buying time on 1 a.m. repeats of *The Insider* and afternoon episodes of *Judge Joe Brown*, instead of spending significantly more on primetime ads, after data indicated that these shows would deliver more swing voters.[52]

Magazines

The number of people reading magazines in the U.S. has remained fairly consistent over the past decade, rising from 211 million in 2012 to 225 million in 2018.[53]

The number of magazines published in the past decade has also remained flat, decreasing from 7,383 in 2008 to 7,218 in 2018. What has declined dramatically is publisher revenues, down to 28 billion in 2017 from 46 billion in 2007.[54]

The secret for print magazines that have survived? Focusing on niche audiences where they can charge marketers higher rates for more qualified targets. They have also cut publication frequency, improved content quality and increased subscriber rates.[55]

For new launches the answer lies in partnering with an existing tribe. In fall of 2016 *The Magnolia Journal,* a lifestyle magazine from Chip and Joanna Gaines, the stars of HGTV's Fixer Upper was launched with a print run of 400,000. Fast forward to 2019, and the magazine now has a rate base of 1.2 million.[56]

But the more common survival strategy for both old and new titles has been for publishers to expand into multi-media properties. In 2018, 42% of U.S. Adults with internet access read a digital magazine up 15% from 2015 (37%).

We are seeing younger age skews among online readers versus those who prefer hard copies. A 2017 report showed that 44.7% of U.S. monthly magazine readers were 55+. For online readers only 29.9% were 55+.[57] And information from *Vogue* magazine about its users indicated that while men read only 12.5% of print copies, they represented 42% of the online audience.[58]

The redefinition of magazine properties as lifestyle brands has led to their expansion into new areas like yoga mats and schools. These days there's a *GQ* Bar in Turkey and a *Vogue* Club in Singapore.[59]

But since many publishers are ill equipped to develop properties beyond magazines and e-zines, other companies have stepped in to help them. In 2019, Authentic Brands Group bought *Sports Illustrated.* Under the terms of the deal, Meredith Corp. will continue publishing the magazine, managing the website, and overseeing marketing. Meanwhile Authentic Brands will focus on licensing opportunities including apparel, sports-gambling and even retail stores. Because as they said "*Sports Illustrated* has real heritage, authenticity and respect."[60]

Newspapers

U.S. newspaper circulation fell in 2018 to its lowest level since 1940, the first year with available data. Newspaper revenues fell from 37.8 billion in 2008 to 14.3 billion in 2018. And newspaper bankruptcy filings continue at a rapid pace with McClatchy, owner of the Miami Herald and Charlotte Observer among others filing in February 2020.[61]

As local and regional newspapers have declined, national newspapers have survived and their audiences have narrowed to feature more affluent readers. The average household income in 2018 for readers of the *New York Times* is $333K, and for *WSJ Magazine* it's $344K, making newspapers a great place to reach the wealthy.[62]

Chapter 15. Objectives, Strategies & Tactics

Strategies are the why, tactics are the how.

The following format is used to express media strategy. As with the format for a creative brief, variations are common. But typically these key elements are included: target audience, consumer insight, objectives, strategies and tactics.

As discussed previously many marketers now target different segments with different campaigns simultaneously, since this allows them to maximize their communication effectiveness.

Let's walk through the format together...

<u>Brand</u>
What brand is the campaign for? (which products, services or ideas?)

While many marketers address the brand as a whole, focusing on specific products or services works as well in media as it does in messaging. Trying to focus on the entire brand can lead to the conundrum of "too many choices." Eliminating some of them becomes the springboard to creativity.

For instance, instead of creating a campaign to sell Snapple, what if you created a campaign to sell Snapple Trop-A-Roca? You might create a campaign based on concert venues, radio promotions and sampling. All these strategies would make sense for a campaign focused on the complete product line too, but the tighter fit with Trop-A-Roca will make for a more engaging and coherent effort.

Background

What will the people executing this plan need to know (about the brand, other marketing efforts, on contract talent, etc.)

The goal is to provide context for the campaign being developed. So this is a good place to include the brand positioning statement.

Celebrities can be used in a variety of ways. If a personality owns the company and must be featured in the campaign (i.e. Goop & Gwyneth Paltrow), this is the time to mention it. Likewise if a celebrity is being used strategically for the brand (i.e., Lincoln & Matthew McConaughey) and should be used in this communication include it here. But any decisions to use celebrities tactically (i.e. for just this campaign) should be included in the tactics section.

Target Audience

Who are we trying to reach? (age, income, marital status, etc.)

As discussed previously, a target definition should include at a minimum -- gender, age range, and a plus one (additional descriptor).

Consumer Insight

What does the target think or feel that we can use to make an emotional connection with them?

The addition of consumer insights to creative briefs took place decades ago. But media planning is often done without consumer insights with media planners focusing solely on efficiencies generated by programmatic buying. This is unfortunate. As we have discussed connections are stronger when commonalities can be identified and exploited.

<u>AT&T Working Woman Grant</u>

To augment its small business user base, AT&T ran a campaign targeting female entrepreneurs. The consumer insight was that women entrepreneurs have a more difficult time raising capital than men. Based on this insight, a $50,000 start-up grant became the centerpiece for the communications plan. The contest was announced in *Working Women* magazine and both AT&T and co-sponsor Deloitte & Touche ran insertions urging women to enter.

Women were invited to send in their business plans, which were then evaluated by volunteers from a local university. Based on their evaluation of the ideas, a winner was selected, and the award and grant money were presented at the annual National Association of Women Business Owners (NAWBO) meeting. Along the way, the company picked up 800 qualified leads.

There is no doubt that the subsequent success of the campaign was because this incentive was perfectly suited to the needs of the target. By recognizing that fact, AT&T was essentially saying we understand you and we know how to help you, and we are going to work for you if you will let us.

Communications Objectives

What is the measurable goal for the campaign? (e.g. increase sales by 10%)

This should be the same objective as was used in the creative brief as the creative strategy and media strategy are working together to achieve it.

In the past, objectives for campaigns were often focused on building awareness. This was measured pre and post effort and if a lift was achieved the campaign was deemed effective. However this changed when we started seeing campaigns that were highly successful at building awareness, but not revenue.

A classic example was the Taco Bell campaign featuring a Chihuahua saying the tagline: "Yo quiero Taco Bell!" The commercial was a fan favorite that was given a guest appearance in the movie *Illegally Blonde.* Sales declined 6% before it was discontinued.[1]

Remember, in order to be perceived as effective, a campaign needs to result in a minimum of a 10% sales increase. If it does not meet this minimum threshold then it is unlikely that it will be repeated.

Communications Strategies

What guiding principles will you use to optimize your specific media selections? (i.e. make them as effective and efficient as possible)

There is great confusion about what constitutes a strategy and what is a tactic. Strategies provide the rationale for tactics.

Consider all the various tactics available. How does one choose which to use?

Research can tell us which tactics are most efficient at reaching our targets. But without coherence tactics are less effective. They work best when they are chosen based on an overlying strategy because then the principles of integrated marketing planning can come into play as the different tactics enhance each other's effectiveness.

For instance a B2B strategy to reach C-titles when they are relaxing could lead to the use of golf tournament sponsorships, *ESPN* and cruise ships as tactics. But if the strategy was to reach C-titles at work, the tactics would more likely be *Wall Street Journal*, *Bloomberg News* and *LinkedIn.*

<u>Secret</u>
P&G's Secret deodorant began supporting the Women's National Soccer team in 2018. It seems like a no brainer. Women who play soccer sweat. That makes them experts on deodorants and antiperspirants - especially those that would work best for women.

Tactics included soccer-themed YouTube videos, and special packaging.

In July 2019, P&G contributed $529,000 to members of the National Soccer team - $23,000 for each of the World Cup-winning players, to highlight the pay difference between men's and women's clubs. And, in September 2019 P&G began buying up to 9,000 seats for soccer teams - 1,000 in each of 9 cities, and donating the seats to women's organizations and sports teams.

Each additional tactic deepened their commitment to the cause and helped increase their bond with the target.[2]

Communications Tactics

What specific media will you use to reach your target? What is your "wow" tactic? (i.e. how will you get their attention?)

We see thousands of communications each day so we have become adept at blocking most of them out. By using tactics that have a specific appeal to an audience you increase the odds that they will actually see and absorb your message. Tailor tactics to your target's preferences, even if they are not your own. Although it may be considered old-fashioned, direct mail is actually a terrific way to reach Adults 65-75 who love to travel and lavish money on the grandkids. While catalogs resonate even with online shoppers.

Tide

In 2018 when Tide decided to win the Super Bowl it employed several different tactics. They started with online teasers, ran commercials on YouTube and posted tweets from influencers including Terry Bradshaw and Betty White. But the "wow" tactic - the one that really got people to notice was the 100 seconds of air time they purchased during the game.

Starting with a :45 second commercial in the first quarter which established the "they're all Tide ads" theme, they had ads in every quarter. This led audiences to play along and speculate as they watched - is this a Tide ad? Given that the Super Bowl is watched in groups who are often more interested in the ads than the game, Tide was able to create an interactive event for viewers. This is likely to have made it even more memorable.

Was it successful? During the game, Tide generated the most online mentions on social media of any brand (164,000). Online the spots have been watched over seven million times.[3]

Chapter 16.
Media Strategy Recommendation.

McCormick Spices Media Strategy Recommendation

Brand

What brand is the campaign for? (which products, services or ideas?)

This campaign is for McCormick Spices. It will address the entire line of products.

Background

What will the people executing this plan need to know (about the brand, other marketing efforts, on contract talent, etc.)

McCormick Spices currently focuses its primary marketing efforts on Women 25-54 with children under 18. We see an opportunity to reach out to Men 18-24 who want to eat healthier, but don't cook, since spices can be sprinkled on takeout and frozen foods, making them both tastier and healthier.

Positioning Statement:
To Men (gender) 18-24 (age range), who want to eat healthy (plus one) but don't cook (consumer insight), McCormick spices (brand) are the perfect solution (key message), because herbs and spices are healthy (reason 1), taste good (reason 2) and are easy to use since you can sprinkle them on your takeout and frozen foods (reason 3)

Target Audience

Who are we trying to reach? (age, income, marital status, etc.)

Men 18-24 who want to eat healthier, but don't cook

See target recommendation and creative brief for details and research support

Consumer Insight

What does the target think or feel that we can use to make an emotional connection with them?

They are members of the Liverpool FC Supporters Club.

Rationale:

1. Liverpool FC has 580 million fans. (Boots, 2015)

2. Men are twice as likely as women to be fans. (Mander, 2005)

3. Liverpool Football Club, founded in 1892, has 300 OLSCs (Official LFC Supporters Clubs) in 90 countries. They meet to watch games live in their own time zones. This means viewing sometimes can and does take place during breakfast. (liverpoolfc.com)

Communications Objectives

What is the measurable goal for the campaign? (e.g. increase sales by 10%)

For the effort to pay out we will need to see a 10% increase in sales by the end of December.

Communications Strategies

What guiding principles will you use to optimize your specific media selections? (i.e. make them as effective and efficient as possible)

Partner with Liverpool Football Club

Communications Tactics

What specific media will you use to reach your target? What is your "wow" tactic? (i.e. how will you get their attention?)

1. Bar collateral & sampling -- table talkers, postcards, and posters will be placed in host bars. Product samples will be available for use and take away.

- Sales at eating and drinking establishments in the US were up more than 4% in 2019, and were predicted to hit a high of $863 billion by year end. (Rogers, 2019)

- 70% of Gen Z says they enjoy going to bars that are different, unique or interesting and 64% are more likely to visit a bar for the experience than purely to get drunk.(Wood, 2019)

- Free samples increase consumers purchasing behavior for as long as 12-months post-sampling. (2018)

2. :15 and :30 video will be placed on game broadcasts -- television and online.

- The Premier League is the most-watched sports league in the world, broadcast in 212 territories to 643 million homes and a potential TV audience of 4.7 billion people. (Wikipedia)

- People 16 - 24 represent 25% of Premier League online soccer viewers and 19% of television soccer viewers. (Mander, 2015)

- As of November 2019, Liverpool FC has 35.4 million followers on Facebook, 20.9 million on Instagram and 12.9 million on Twitter. (2019) And their official YouTube channel has over 1 million subscribers. (2018)

3. Signage at worldwide pre-season summer tour venues in the US.

- In 2018, Liverpool's pre-season tour drew 52,000 attendees in New Jersey and 51,000 in attendees in North Carolina. In 2019, it drew 40,361 attendees in Indiana (Notre Dame) (Berardino, 2019), 31,112 in NYC (2019), and 35,654 in Boston. (Bird, 2019)

- Research has shown that brands promoted at sporting events can see a lift of 8.4% within 48 hours of the game. (Troianovski, 2013)

- Liverpool FC's dedicated channel -- LFCTV, is available on Sky and Virgin Media in the UK and

Ireland, and on Turner Sports B/R Live. Elsewhere access is video-on-demand. (2019)

Next Steps

Pending agreement to this recommendation, we will begin media plan development.

Boots, B. (2015, December 18) Liverpool have the 2nd most fans in the world, study says. *empireofthekop.com* Retrieved May 31, 2020, from https://www.empireofthekop.com/2015/12/18/liverpool-have-the-2nd-most-fans-in-the-world-study-says/

Mander, J. & McGrath, F. (2015, March) Premier League Fans Summary. *globalwebindex.net.* Retrieved May 31, 2020, from https://insight.globalwebindex.net/hs-fs/hub/304927/file-2593818997-

https://www.liverpoolfc.com/fans/official-lfc-supporters-clubs

Rogers, K. (2019, August 19) Restaurant spending set to hit high in 2019 as consumers spend more of their budget on dining out. *cnbc.com.* Retrieved May 31, 2020 , from https://www.cnbc.com/2019/08/19/americans-putting-more-of-their-budget-toward-eating-out.html

Wood, J. (2019, March 26) Last orders: how can alcohol brands and bars respond to declining interest in Gen Z? *Opinium.* Retrieved May 31, 2020, from https://www.thedrum.com/opinion/2019/03/26/last-orders-how-can-alcohol-brands-and-bars-respond-declining-interest-gen-z

(2018, June 20) Product Sampling: The Research Behind the Results. *sonasmarketing.com.* Retrieved May 31, 2020, from https://www.sonasmarketing.com/blog/product-sampling-the-research-behind-the-results

https://en.wikipedia.org/wiki/Premier_League

Mander, J. & McGrath, F. (2015, March) Premier League Fans Summary. *globalwebindex.net.* Retrieved May 31, 2020, from https://insight.globalwebindex.net/hs-fs/hub/304927/file-2593818997-
(2019, November) Number of social media followers of Liverpool in November 2019, by platform. *statista.com.* Retrieved May 31, 2020, from https://www.statista.com/statistics/964294/liverpool-facebook-instagram-twitter-social-media-following/

(2018, May 7) Liverpool FC's official YouTube channel has hit one million subscribers. *liverpoolfc.com.* Retrieved June 1, 2020, from https://www.liverpoolfc.com/news/announcements/301043-liverpool-fc-youtube-one-million

Berardino, M. (2019, July 19) Borussia Dortmund defeat Liverpool FC in half-filled Notre Dame Stadium. *indystar.com.* Retrieved May 31, 2020, from https://www.indystar.com/story/sports/2019/07/19/borussia-dortmund-defeat-liverpool-fc-half-filled-notre-dame-stadium/1734212001/

(2019, July 25) Liverpool vs Sporting 2019 Attendance 31,112.*blogger.com.* Retrieved May 31, 2020, from http://www.soccer-blogger.com/2019/07/25/liverpool-vs-sporting-lisbon-2019-attendance-31112-yankee-stadium-2-2-highlights-origi-wijnaldum-mignolet-error-video/

Bird, H. (2019, July 22) Anfield comes to Fenway: Liverpool fans in Boston made the Champions League winners feel right at home. *boston.com.* Retrieved May 31, 2020, from https://www.boston.com/sports/soccer/2019/07/22/liverpool-fenway-park-jurgen-klopp-boston

Troianovski, A. (2013, May 21) Phone Firms Sell Data on Customers. *wsj.com.* Retrieved May 28, 2020, from https://www.wsj.com/articles/SB10001424127887323463704578497153556847658

(2019, September 19) B/R Live to Exclusively Distribute Liverpool's 24/7 TV Channel in U.S. *WarnerMedia.* retrieved June 1, 2020, from https://pressroom.warnermediagroup.com/ca/media-release/turner-sports/br-live-exclusively-distribute-liverpools-247-tv-channel-us

Chapter 17.
Final Strategy Recommendation

When developing a marketing plan the first step is to identify the target audience. After that a positioning statement is developed so that the complete marketing proposition is available for reference.

The next step is to put together the media strategy. For simplicity's sake, the example in this book includes one objective and one strategy with three tactics. Typically a plan would include one objective and three strategies, each with three tactics. As mentioned previously it may be necessary to develop multiple creative briefs depending upon the media strategies.

If all documentation is presented simultaneously, the research support provided for each section can be edited to eliminate duplication as can the inclusion of the positioning statement in the media strategy recommendation. But typically each document is discussed in a separate meeting so that the process can be made more collaborative, which leads to more successful results.

Afterward

Consumer behavior not only affects what we buy, it also affects how we think and feel.

This book was finished on July 4, 2020. As of today 2.8 million Americans have been infected with Covid-19, and over 129,000 have died from it. Infections are surging - up 90% in the past two weeks thanks to people refusing to stay home and wear masks.

It seems probable that some of these misguided actions are due to tribal affiliations with Donald Trump, Republicans and Fox News. All of whom are pretending that neither staying home nor wearing masks is necessary.

But given that all decisions are emotional, we need to consider that those who refuse to stay home and wear masks are motivated by fear.

They believe that as long as they continue to pretend everything is normal it will be. Wearing a mask and staying home crushes that fantasy. It is an acknowledgement that Covid-19 is a deadly disease that can kill them or their loved ones. It doesn't get much scarier than that. And it's hard to be in denial when you are wearing a mask.

The research about measles vaccinations suggests the only way to drive compliance is to scare people even more by showing them visuals of those dying from Covid-19. But will we as a society be willing to do this?

To continue the dialog about how consumer behavior impacts persuasion and marketing, please feel free to follow Prof. Lehrer's blog, published weekly, syndicated by Newstex/ACI Information Group.

http://pjlehrer.blogspot.com/

Glossary

80/20 rule: Marketing principle formulated by Joseph Juran, which states that in any given category, 20% of the people account for 80% of the revenue.

Acquiescence bias: When people say what others want to hear in order to be agreeable.

A&U: Attitude & Usage – broad omnibus research study that seeks to determine underlying trends for categories and products.

Art director: The member of the creative development team who is primarily responsible for visuals.

Baby Boomers: People born from 1946 -- 1964.

Bleed: When the live area of a 2-D creative piece extends to the outer edges of the page.

Brand: The space a product or service occupies in the consumer's mind.

B2B: Business-to-business.

Conformity cues: Looking at the behavior of others.

Cognitive dissonance: When new information conflicting with a belief results in discomfort.

Consumer Insight: Something the target thinks or feels that can be used to make an emotional connection with them.

Covid-19: Novel coronavirus that caused a global pandemic in 2020.

CPM: Cost-per-thousand – calculated using the following formula: *CPM = (Cost of media buy/Total impressions) x 1000.*

CPMs are used to compare different media properties based on cost efficiency.

Creative Brief: Format used to convey message strategy.

Demographics: Population or consumer statistics regarding socioeconomic factors such as age, income, sex, occupation, education, family size and the like.

Descriptor: Demographic, psychographic or behavioral aspect that pertains to a specific target.

Differentiator: A specific aspect of a target, product or service that distinguishes it from the competition.

Ebbinghaus Forgetting Curve: Demonstrates that without reminders learning retention drops to 21% in 31 days, but with three reminders spaced within ten days, retention rises to 75%.

Editorial adjacencies: Running an advertisement next to compatible editorial.

Flighting: Scheduling advertising in an off again on again pattern in order to achieve continuity with a limited budget.

Focus groups: Groups of 6–12 individuals who respond to specific stimuli, and provide open-ended feedback guided by a moderator, whose role is to minimize group think and maximize individual participation.

FOMO: Fear of missing out. (see loss aversion)

Framing: The context provided for information, which influences how it is perceived.

Frequency: The average number of times that someone in the target market will see campaign communications.

Generation Alpha: Potential name for people born after 2012. End date not yet determined.

Gen X: People born from 1965 -- 1980.

Gen Y: (Also called Millennials) People born from 1981 – 1996.

Gen Z: People born from 1997 - 2012.

Heavy-up: Concentrating advertising over a specific time period in order to create more impact.

Heavy users: Individuals who are part of the 20% of users who account for 80% of volume (See 80/20 rule).

Illusionary Truth Effect: After three exposures, people believe that something is true even if it isn't.

IMC: Integrated Marketing Communications – using a variety of media types in a coordinated communications effort.

Impressions: The raw number of exposures for a communications effort. Since the number includes multiple exposures, it does not accurately portray the number of individuals exposed.

Incidental emotions: Emotions that do not relate to the matter at hand, but still influence decision-making and behavior.

Informational Conformity: Observing majority behavior.

Integral emotions: Emotions that relate directly to the matter at hand.

Key message: The singular thought to be communicated in a positioning statement or creative strategy.

Loss aversion: Avoiding/fearing risk because people hate to lose what they have more than they like to win.

Mass media: Media that reaches large amounts of people; typically includes network television, outdoor, monthly magazines, and national buys of radio and newspapers.

Millennials: (Also called Gen Y) People born from 1981 – 1996.

Minimum communication thresholds: The amount of repetitions necessary to create awareness, understanding and persuasion.

Myers-Briggs (MBTI): Personality profiling system developed in 1943 used to understand differences in behavior among people.

Niche media: Highly targeted, low-out-of-pocket media used to reach a specific niche target.

Niche target: A small well-defined segment with strong commonalities that make them more likely to purchase a brand, and easy to reach efficiently with targeted media

Objective: The specific measurable goal for a marketing effort.

Objectives, strategies and tactics: Format used to convey media strategy.

Pew research: Leading publisher of research information. Designated generational parameters.

Plus one: A descriptor that is unique to a target audience that can help to create connections with them.

Positional Concerns: Measuring oneself based on the achievement of peers.

Positioning statement: A standard format used to express strategy.

To ____*(target market: gender, age range, plus one)*____,and/but ____*(consumer insight)*____, Brand XYZ ____*(product or service)*____, is ____*(key message)*____, because ____*(3 reasons to believe)*____.

Primacy effect: The tendency to believe that the first thing we hear about a subject is true.

Primary research: Research that is generated and paid for by a specific company.

Primary target: The segment of users designated as the most important to marketers -- typically the heavy user as defined by the 80/20 rule.

Product placement: Integration of product promotion into content.

Provincial norms: Behavior that is shared by people who live in similar circumstances.

Psychographics: Criteria for segmenting consumers by lifestyle, attitudes, beliefs, values, personality, buying motives, and/or extent of product usage.

Qualitative research: Research that allows subjects to provide open-ended answers; typically takes the form of focus groups.

Quantitative research: Research that is formatted so that responses can be tallied and evaluated. Statistically significant populations are used so that data may be accurately projected nationally.

Reach: The percentage of the target market that will see the campaign.

Recency theory: Running a low level of communications consistently throughout the year to constantly remind the consumer of a product or service's existence. Most frequently used for well established brands with flat seasonality.

Richard Thaler: 2017 Nobel Prize winner who showed that behavior that might seem irrational is in fact predictable based on human behavior research.

ROI: Return on investment.

Roll-out: Advertising a product or service in a limited geographical region, and then gradually adding new markets over time. Generally used when manufacturing capabilities limit the ability to launch a product nationally.

Rule of Threes: Consumers need to be exposed to an idea three times before they remember it.

Secondary research: Research that is done by a third party.

Secondary user: An alternative to the primary user, which typically does not yield as much revenue, but can still be profitable. Often a niche target.

Silent Generation: People born from 1928 – 1945.

Social proof: Choosing to align with the majority opinion.

Spot media: Media placed in individual markets.

Statistically significant: Data from a sample size that is large enough to be projected nationally with accuracy.

Storyboard: Visual representation of broadcast creative which includes key visuals and complete copy.

Strategy: Why you are doing something -- the underlying reason behind the selection of specific tactics.

Support (reasons to believe): Specifics that provide the rationale for the key message in positioning statements and creative briefs.

Syndication: Television shows that run nationally on different networks locally, often at different times as well. Examples include: *Wheel of Fortune* and *Jeopardy.*

Tactics: The specific actions taken based on the guidance of the strategy.

Target market: A group of people that a piece of communications is designed to reach. Sometimes referred to as "persona."

Target segment: A specific portion of a larger target market that shares commonalities.

Tribe: A group of people who share common interests and attitudes.

Triple-bid: Asking three vendors to provide specs and costs for a job, so that approaches and prices can be compared.

Turn-key: A complete package that provides all the elements necessary for the project so that it can be implemented with little additional effort on the part of the purchaser.

Unconscious bias: Preferences based on genetics and environment that the holder is unaware of.

Visual Word Form Area (VWFA): Area of the brain which converts words to pictures which we then store for quicker access.

VNR (Video News Release): Marketer generated communications, designed to appear as content, and integrated into news programming without attribution.

Wear-out: When a piece of communications has run so frequently that is it no longer effective.

"Wow" tactic: A specific communications tactic that will allow the campaign to breakthrough clutter, and capture the interest of the target market.

References

Chapter 1

[1] Brandt, A. (2012, January) Inventing Conflicts of Interest: A History of Tobacco Industry Tactics. *nih.gov.* Retrieved February 28, 2020, from https://www.ncbi.nlm.nih.gov/pmc/articles/PMC3490543/

[2] (2019) Master Settlement Agreement. *publichealthlawcenter.org.* Retrieved February 28, 2020, from https://publichealthlawcenter.org/topics/commercial-tobacco-control/commercial-tobacco-control-litigation/master-settlement-agreement

[3]3 Wolfers, J. (2016, January 10) When Teamwork Doesn't Work for Women. *nytimes.com.* Retrieved May 1, 2020, from https://www.nytimes.com/2016/01/10/upshot/when-teamwork-doesnt-work-for-women.html

[4] Lerchenmueller, M., Sorenson, O. & Jena, A. (2019, November 11) Gender differences in how scientists present the importance of their research: observational study. *bmj.com.* Retrieved May 1, 2020, from https://www.bmj.com/content/bmj/367/bmj.l6573.full.pdf

[5] Mullainathan, S. (2019, December 8) Biased Algorithms Are Easier to Fix Than Biased People. *nytimes.com.* Retrieved February 26, 2020, from https://www.nytimes.com/2019/12/06/business/algorithm-bias-fix.html

[6] Russonello, G. (2019, November 24) Four Problems With 2016 Polling That Could Play Out Again in 2020. *nytimes.com.* Retrieved February 26, 2020, from https://www.nytimes.com/2019/11/23/us/politics/2020-trump-presidential-polls.html

[7] (2006, May 15) Studies: People Generally Lie to Preserve Self-Esteem. *foxnews.com.* retrieved May 3, 2016, from http://www.foxnews.com/story/2006/05/15/studies-people-generally-lie-to-preserve-self-esteem.html

[8] (2006, March 13) Nobody Here (Almost) But Us Healthy Eaters! *Adweek* p34.

[9] Aydinoglu, N., & Krishna, A. (2014, July) Imagining thin: Why vanity sizing works. *Journal of Psychology.* Retrieved April 23, 2020, from https://www.sciencedirect.com/science/article/abs/pii/S1057740811001148

[10] Sarniak, R. (2015, August) 9 types of research bias and how to avoid them. *quirks.com.* Retrieved May 1, 2020, from https://www.quirks.com/articles/9-types-of-research-bias-and-how-to-avoid-them

[11] (2020) Questionnaire Design. *pewresearch.org.* Retrieved February 28, 2020, from https://www.pewresearch.org/methods/u-s-survey-research/questionnaire-design/

[12] Thomson-DeVeaux, A. (2019, July 15) Americans Say They Would Vote Foe A Woman, But... *fivethirtyeight.com.* Retrieved February 28, 2020, from https://fivethirtyeight.com/features/americans-say-they-would-vote-for-a-woman-but/

[13] Zukin, C. (2015, June 20) What's the Matter With Polling? *nytimes.com.* Retrieved May 3, 2016, from http://www.nytimes.com/2015/06/21/opinion/sunday/whats-the-matter-with-polling.html

[14] Thakkar, V. (2020, April 16) Vitamin D And Covid Disparities. *wsj.com.* Retrieved April 24, 2020, fromhttps://www.wsj.com/articles/vitamin-d-and-coronavirus-disparities-11587078141

Chapter 2

[1] Karp, H. (2015, November 20) The typical Adele Fan? A Soccer-Playing Mom. *The Wall Street Journal* pD1.

[2] Barovick, H., Cruz, G., Salemme, C., Sharples, T., Silver, A., & Stinchfield, K. (2008, March 17) Milestones. *Time.*

[3] McGraw, E. (2020, June 5) A few superspreaders transmit the majority of coronavirus cases. *theconversation.com.* retrieved June 6, 2020, from https://theconversation.com/a-few-superspreaders-transmit-the-majority-of-coronavirus-cases-139950

[4] Del Vecchio, G. (2014, May 12) Got Milk? Got Fired: 5 Valuable Lessons That All Executives Must Heed. *huffpost.com.* Retrieved April 27, 2020, from https://www.huffpost.com/entry/got-milk-got-fired-5-valu_b_4938176

[5] Pregnancy Symptoms & Solutions. (2009) w*hattoexpect.com.* Retrieved January 21, 2009, from http://www.whattoexpect.com/pregnancy/symptoms-and-solutions/hemorrhoids.aspx

[6] Drinking Juice Slashes Alzheimer's (2006) *Fisher Center for Alzheimer's Research Foundation.* Retrieved September 15, 2006, from http://www.alzinfo.org/newsarticle/templates/newstemplate.asp?articleid=3&zoneid=1

[7] Gonzalez, D. & Pardilla, A. (2019, December 30) Blue Apron Now Has A Weight Watchers Meal Plan. *huffpost.com.* Retrieved May 1, 2020, from https://www.huffpost.com/entry/blue-apron-now-has-a-weight-watchers-meal-plan-partnership_n_5c1bde94e4b0407e907881f4

[8] Fels, A. (2019, January 10) Mount Sinai Health System and Epicured Partner to Bring Culinary Cures to Patients. *mountsinai.org* retrieved May 1, 2020, from https://www.mountsinai.org/about/newsroom/2019/mount-sinai-health-system-and-epicured-partner-to-bring-culinary-cures-to-patients

[9] Bruell, A. (2018, May 20) Northwestern Mutual Gets Results From Ads That Talk to Women. *wsj.com.* Retrieved March 3, 2020, from https://www.wsj.com/articles/northwestern-mutual-gets-results-from-ads-that-talk-to-women-1526868660

[10] Petersen, A. (2015, October 1) Secrets of a Hotel Test Lab. *The Wall Street Journal.* p D1

[11] Lyttle, J. (2001, April) The Effectiveness of Humor in Persuasion: The Case of Business Ethnics Training. *The Journal of General Psychology.* Retrieved April 24, 2020, from http://www.jimlyttle.com/PDF/JGP.pdf

[12] MacDonald, F. (2016, September 26) Two More Classic Psychology Studies Just Failed The Reproducibility Test. *sciencealert.com.* Retrieved April 24, 2020, from https://www.sciencealert.com/two-more-classic-psychology-studies-just-failed-the-reproducibility-test

[13] Fry, R. (2020, April 28) Millennials overtake Baby Boomers as America's largest generation. *pewresearch.org.* Retrieved May 11, 2020, from https://www.pewresearch.org/fact-tank/2020/04/28/millennials-overtake-baby-boomers-as-americas-largest-generation/

[14] (2017, April 24) Millennial Females' 20 Biggest Passions Right Now. *ypulse.com.* Retrieved April 1, 2020, from https://www.ypulse.com/article/2017/04/24/millennial-females-20-biggest-passions-right-now/

[15] Satagaj, R., Walsh, K., Aiello, M., Larcom, A. & Valerio, R. (2020, January 7) Retrieved April 1, 2020, from https://www.ihrsa.org/improve-your-club/industry-news/2019-fitness-industry-trends-shed-light-on-2020-beyond/

[16] Gurrentz, B. (2018, November 15) For Young Adults, Cohabitation Is Up, Marriage Is Down. *census.gov.* Retrieved April 1, 2020, from https://www.census.gov/library/stories/2018/11/cohabitaiton-is-up-marriage-is-down-for-young-adults.html

[17] Weller, J. (2019, November 11) 10 Gym Membership Statistics You Need To Know. *glofox.com.* Retrieved April 1, 2020, from https://www.glofox.com/blog/10-gym-membership-statistics-you-need-to-know/

[18] Dictionary of marketing terms. (2009). *allbusiness.com.* Retrieved January 20, 2009, from http://www.allbusiness.com/glossaries/demographics/4963084-1.html

[19] Dictionary of marketing terms. (2009). *allbusiness.com.* Retrieved January 20, 2009, from http://www.allbusiness.com/glossaries/psychographics/4956688-1.html

Chapter 3

[1] Junge, C. (2011, May 24) How your friends make you fat - the social network of weight. *harvard.edu.* Retrieved March 3, 2020, from https://www.health.harvard.edu/blog/how-your-friends-make-you-fat%E2%80%94the-social-network-of-weight-201105242666

[2] http://ads.manhattanministorage.com/occupy-us/many-rooms/

[3] Rahim, Z. (2020, June 1) Thousands around the world protest George Floyd's death in global display of solidarity. *cnn.com*. Retrieved June 1, 2020, from https://www.cnn.com/2020/06/01/world/george-floyd-global-protests-intl/index.html

[4] Bohner, G. & Schluter, L. (2014, August 1) A Room with a Viewpoint Revisited: Descriptive Norms and Hotel Guests' Towel Reuse Behavior. *nih.gov*. Retrieved April 28, 2020, from https://www.ncbi.nlm.nih.gov/pmc/articles/PMC4118982/

[5] Akst, D. (2016, July 16) Want to Build Trust? Order the Same Food. *wsj.com*. Retrieved April 27, 2020, from https://www.wsj.com/articles/want-to-build-trust-order-the-same-food-1468508945

[6] Frey, W. (2018, March 14) The US will become 'minority white' in 2045, Census projccts. *brookings.edu*. Retrieved March 3, 2020, from https://www.brookings.edu/blog/the-avenue/2018/03/14/the-us-will-become-minority-white-in-2045-census-projects/

[7] Lopez, G., Cilluffo, A. & Patten, E. (2017, September 8) Indians in the US Fact Sheet. *pewresearch.org*. Retrieved March 3, 2020, from https://www.pewsocialtrends.org/fact-sheet/asian-americans-indians-in-the-u-s/

[8] Imada, T., Carlson, S., & Itakura, S. (2013, March 16) East-West Cultural Differences in Context-sensitivity are Evident in Early Childhood. *nih.gov*. Retrieved March 19, 2020, from https://www.ncbi.nlm.nih.gov/pmc/articles/PMC5877415/

[9] (2020) Pet Industry Market Size & Ownership Statistics. *American Pet Products Association*. Retrieved June 9, 2020, from https://www.americanpetproducts.org/press_industrytrends.asp#:~:text=2018%20%2490.5%20(2018%20figures%20have,using%20APPA's%20new%20research%20methodology.)&text=In%202019%2C%20%2495.7%20billion%20was%20spent%20on%20our%20pets%20in%20the%20U.S.&text=For%202020%2C%20it%20estimated%20that,our%20pets%20in%20the%20U.S.

[10] Gazdik, T. (2015, August 20) Americans' Spending Proves Love Of Pets. *mediapos.com*. Retrieved May 5, 2016, from http://www.mediapost.com/publications/article/256552/americans-spending-proves-love-of-

pets.html?utm_source=newsletter&utm_medium=email&utm_content=headline&utm_campaign=85468

[11] Settembre, J. (2015, September 13) Canine Cuisine. *The New York Daily News.* p13

[12] Irwin, T. (2014, June 20) PetSmart Charities, Match.com Pair For Dating Events. *mediapost.com.* Retrieved June 20, 2014, from http://www.mediapost.com/publications/article/228365/petsmart-charities-matchcom-pair-for-dating-even.html

[13] Mayyasi, A & Priceonomics (2016, June 22) How Subarus Came to Be Seen as Cars for Lesbians. *theatlantic.com.* retrieved March 3, 2020, from https://www.theatlantic.com/business/archive/2016/06/how-subarus-came-to-be-seen-as-cars-for-lesbians/488042/

[14] Kapner, S. (2018, June 20) Marriage Is Out of Fashion. So Why Is Tiffany Selling More Engagement Rings? *wsj.com.* Retrieved March 3, 2020, from https://www.wsj.com/articles/marriage-is-out-of-fashion-so-why-is-tiffany-selling-more-engagement-rings-1529487001

[15] Needleman, S. (2015, October 12) How Videogames Are Saving The Symphony Orchestra. *wsj.com.* Retrieved March 3, 2020, from https://www.wsj.com/articles/how-videogames-are-saving-the-symphony-orchestra-1444696737

[16] Tarmy, J. (2018, October 11) The Most-Visited Exhibition in Met Museum History. *bloomberg.com.* Retrieved March 3, 2020, from https://www.bloomberg.com/news/articles/2018-10-11/heavenly-bodies-was-the-met-s-most-visited-exhibition-ever

[17] Catton, P. (2016, November 27) Broadway Casts Offer Retailers a New Stage. *wsj.com.* Retrieved March 6, 2020, from https://www.wsj.com/articles/broadway-casts-offer-retailers-a-new-stage-1480292624

[18] Passy, C. (2017, February 5) 'Waitress' Fans Vie For a Chance to Sing Along. *wsj.com.* Retrieved March 6, 2020, from https://www.wsj.com/articles/waitress-fans-vie-for-chance-to-sing-along-1486341448

[19] Chipkin, H. (2019, January 17) Partnerships Help Hyatt Differentiate Brands. *mediapost.com.* Retrieved May 15, 2020, from

https://www.mediapost.com/publications/article/330706/partnerships-help-hyatt-differentiate-brands.html

Chapter 5

[1] Buchanan, T. (2008, March 6) Retrieval of Emotional Memories. *nih.gov.* Retrieved May 30, 2016, from http://www.ncbi.nlm.nih.gov/pmc/articles/PMC2265099/

[2] Kensinger, E. (2007) Negative Emotion Enhances Memory Accuracy. *Association for Psychological Science.* Retrieved May 30, 2016, from https://www2.bc.edu/elizabeth-kensinger/Kensinger_CD07.pdf

[3] Lerner, J., Valdesolo, P., & Kassam. K. (2014, June 16) Emotion and Decision-Making. *Annual Review of Psychology.* Retrieved March 21, 2020, from https://www.annualreviews.org/doi/full/10.1146/annurev-psych-010213-115043

[4] Baumeister, R., Bratslavsky, E., Finkenauer, F. & Vohs, K. (2001) Bad Is Stronger Than Good. *Review of General Psychology.* Retrieved May 29, 2016, from http://dev.rickhanson.net/wp-content/files/papers/BadStrongerThanGood.pdf

[5] Berger, J. (2020, May 18) How To Change Anyone's Mind. *wsj.com.* Retrieved May 18, 2020, from https://www.wsj.com/articles/how-to-change-anyones-mind-11582301073

[6] Irwin, N. (2018, July 14) Two Words That Could Shape the Politics of the Trade War: Loss Aversion. *nytimes.com.* Retrieved March 13, 2020, from https://www.nytimes.com/2018/07/13/upshot/trade-war-loss-aversion.html

[7] The Rule of Scarcity - Get Anyone to Take Immediate Action. *Westside Toastmasters.* Retrieved June 2, 2016, from http://westsidetoastmasters.com/resources/laws_persuasion/chap1.html

[8] Passy, C. (2019, August 19) Final Bows Boost Broadway Ticket Sales. *wsj.com.* Retrieved May 29, 2020, from https://www.wsj.com/articles/final-bows-boost-broadway-ticket-sales-11566255731

[9] Patel, M., Asch, D., and K. Volpp. (2016, March 6) Paying Employees to Lose Weight. *The New York Times.* p10.

[10] Bowles, S. (2009, March) When Economic Incentives Backfire. *hbr.org.* Retrieved March 25, 2020, from https://hbr.org/2009/03/when-economic-incentives-backfire

[11] Terada, Y. (2019, July 25) Extrinsic Motivation: It Might Be Even Worse Than You Thought. *edutopia.org.* Retrieved March 25, 2020, from https://www.edutopia.org/article/extrinsic-motivation-it-might-be-even-worse-you-thought

[12] Renaud, K. (2019, September 18) People Need an Incentive to Use Strong Passwords. We Gave Them One. *wsj.com.* Retrieved May 14, 2020, from https://www.wsj.com/articles/people-need-an-incentive-to-use-strong-passwords-we-gave-them-one-11568734702

[13] Pinker, S. (2016, March 12) The Fear Factor Sells Vaccines Against Measles. *The Wall Street Journal.* pC2.

[14] Oychyl, T. (2008, June 7) Goal Progress and Happiness. *psychologytoday.com.* Retrieved May 8, 2016, from https://www.psychologytoday.com/blog/dont-delay/200806/goal-progress-and-happiness

[15] Houston, E. (2020, April 15) What is Goal Setting and How to Do It Well. *positivepsychology.com.* Retrieved May 18, 2020, from https://positivepsychology.com/goal-setting/

[16] Blackman, A. (2014, November 10) Can Money Buy You Happiness? *wsj.com.* Retrieved May 8, 2016, from http://www.wsj.com/articles/can-money-buy-happiness-heres-what-science-has-to-say-1415569538

[17] Gilovich, T., Kumar, A., & Jampol, L. (2014, August 20) A wonderful life: experiential consumption and the pursuit of happiness. *Journal of Consumer Psychology.* Retrieved May 18, 2020, from https://static1.squarespace.com/static/5394dfa6e4b0d7fc44700a04/t/547d589ee4b04b0980670fee/1417500830665/Gilovich%20Kumar%20Jampol%20(in%20press)%20A%20Wonderful%20Life%20JCP.pdf?mod=article_inline

[18] https://en.wikiquote.org/wiki/Theodore_Roosevelt

[19] Perry, S. (2018, October 17) Social class affects whether buying things or experiences makes you happier, study suggests. *minnpost.com.* Retrieved March 13, 2020, from https://www.minnpost.com/second-opinion/2018/10/social-class-affects-whether-buying-things-or-experiences-makes-you-happier-study-suggests/

[20] (2014, July) Millennials Fueling The Economy Experience. *eventbrite.com.* retrieved May 18, 2020, from http://eventbrite-s3.s3.amazonaws.com/marketing/Millennials_Research/Gen_PR_Final.pdf

[21] Wexler, A. (2016, December 30) Vineyard Gets Its Ducks in a Row and Visitors Flock In. *wsj.com.* Retrieved May 18, 2020, from https://www.wsj.com/articles/a-vineyard-gets-its-ducks-in-a-row-and-visitors-flock-in-1483026195

[22] Strohmetz, D., Rind, B., Fisher, R. & Lynn, M. (2002) Sweetening the till: The use of candy to increase restaurant tipping. *Journal of Applied Social Psychology.* Retrieved May 20, 2020, from https://scholarship.sha.cornell.edu/cgi/viewcontent.cgi?referer=&httpsredir=1&article=1129&context=articles

[23] Passy, C. (2020, January 5) Blue Eggs and Salt? Restaurant Freebies Get Fancy. *wsj.com.* Retrieved May 20, 2020, from https://www.wsj.com/articles/restaurants-eat-the-cost-to-give-diners-free-treats-11578236400

[24] Howard, D. (1992) *Journal of Consumer Psychology.* Retrieved April 28, 2020, from https://www.jstor.org/stable/1480584?seq=8#metadata_info_tab_contents

[25] Ariely, D. (2020, January 4) Ask Ariely: On Team Tragedy, Airport Anxiety, and Grumpy Gift-wrapping. *danariely.com.* Retrieved April 28, 2020, from http://danariely.com/2020/01/04/ask-ariely-on-team-tragedy-airport-anxiety-and-grumpy-gift-wrapping/

[26] Koh, Y. (2019, December 23) Walmart, Target Embrace 8-Year-Old YouTube Influencer's Brand. *wsj.com.* Retrieved April 28, 2020, from https://www.wsj.com/articles/walmart-target-embrace-8-year-old-youtube-influencers-brand-11577105971?mod=article_inline

[27] Dunn, E. & Norton, M. (2012, July 7) Don't Indulge. Be Happy. *nytimes.com.* Retrieved May 8, 2016, from http://www.nytimes.com/2012/07/08/opinion/sunday/dont-indulge-be-happy.html?_r=0

[28] Whillans, A., Dunn, E., Smeets, P., Bekkers, R., & Norton, M. (2017, August 8) Buying Time Promotes Happiness. *Proceedings of the National Academy of Sciences.* Retrieved April 27, 2020, from https://www.pnas.org/content/114/32/8523.full

[29] Zaslow, A. (2006, March 18) Happiness Inc. *wsj.com.* Retrieved May 8, 2016, from http://www.wsj.com/articles/SB114263698678301765

[30] Reynolds, G. (2015, June 25) The Joy of (Just the Right Amount of) Sex. *wsj.com.* http://well.blogs.nytimes.com/2015/06/25/the-joy-of-just-the-right-amount-of-sex/?WT.mc_id=2015-KWP-AUD_DEV&WT.mc_ev=click&ad-keywords=AUDDEVREMARK&kwp_0=22265&kwp_4=146673&kwp_1=161582&_r=3

[31] Stephens-Davidowitz, S. (2015, January 24) Searching for Sex. *nytimes.com.* Retrieved May 9, 2016, from http://www.nytimes.com/2015/01/25/opinion/sunday/seth-stephens-davidowitz-searching-for-sex.html?_r=0

[32] Dunn, E., Aknin, L., and Norton, M. (2015, September 5) Prosocial Spending and Happiness: Using Money to Benefit Others Pays Off. *harvard.edu.* Retrieved May 9, 2016, from http://nrs.harvard.edu/urn-3:HUL.InstRepos:11189976

[33] Ganguly, P. (2018, February 5) Studying empathy can sometimes seem like a look at how self-involved we are. *massivesci.com.* Retrieved May 6, 2020, from https://massivesci.com/articles/empathy-bias-produce-groups-emotions/

[34] Newman, A. (2019, July 21) What Our Reporter Learned Delivering Burritos to New Yorkers. *nytimes.com.* Retrieved October 2, 2019, from https://www.nytimes.com/2019/07/21/reader-center/insider-reporter-food-deliveryman.html

[35] Baar, A. (2008, March 12) Pedigree Adoption Campaign Drives Dog Food Sales. *mediapost.com.* Retrieved May 6, 2020, from https://www.mediapost.com/publications/article/78294/pedigree-adoption-campaign-drives-dog-food-sales.html

[36] Vranica, S. (2008, December 22) Dog-Food Ad to Try a New Trick. *wsj.com.* retrieved May 6, 2020, from https://www.wsj.com/articles/SB122990008468524941
[37] Bernstein, E. (2016, April 19) Why Making New Friends Is Harder for Grown-Ups. *The Wall Street Journal.* p D1.

[38] Agronin, M. (2016, March) It's Time to Rethink The Bucket-List Retirement. *Wall Street Journal* pR2

[39] Sanghani, R. (2014, December 28) Generation Lonely: Britain's young people have never been less connected. *telegraph.co.uk.* Retrieved May 8, 2016, from http://www.telegraph.co.uk/women/womens-life/11312075/Generation-Lonely-Britains-young-people-have-never-been-less-connected.html

[40] Clements, J. (2008, April 2) Down the Tube: the Sad Stats On Happiness, Money and TV. *wsj.com.* retrieved May 8, 2018, from http://www.wsj.com/articles/SB120709012659781613

[41] Williams, J. (2018, July 9) The Elites Feed Anti-Immigrant Bias *wsj.com* Retrieved March 18, 2020, from https://www.wsj.com/articles/the-elites-feed-anti-immigrant-bias-1531176949

[42] Day, C. (2019, August 25) Americans Have Shifted Dramatically on What Values Matter Most.*wsj.com.* Retrieved March 18, 2020, from https://www.wsj.com/articles/americans-have-shifted-dramatically-on-what-values-matter-most-11566738001

[43] Kapner, S. & Chinni, D. (2019, November 19) Are Your Jeans Red or Blue? Shopping America's Partisan Divide. *wsj.com.* Retrieved April 24, 2020, from https://www.wsj.com/articles/are-your-jeans-red-or-blue-shopping-americas-partisan-divide-11574185777

[44] Hoover, A. (2017, January 10) Is it fair to boycott L.L. Bean over Donald Trump donation? *csmonitor.com.* Retrieved March 18, 2020, from https://www.csmonitor.com/USA/2017/0110/Is-it-fair-to-boycott-L.L.-Bean-over-Donald-Trump-donation

[45] Shvedsky, L. (2018, November 11) Patagonia 's CEO is donating company's entire $10M Trump tax cut to fight climate change. *upworthy.com.* Retrieved March 18, 2020, from

https://www.upworthy.com/patagonia-s-ceo-is-donating-company-s-entire-10-m-trump-tax-cut-to-fight-climate-change

[46] Peters, A. (2019, May 17) Inside Levi's stand against gun violence. *fastcompany.com.* Retrieved April24, 2020, from https://www.fastcompany.com/90346594/inside-levis-stand-against-gun-violence

[47] Mahoney, S. (2018, October 10) Levi's Credits Activism With Surging Sales. *mediapost.com.* Retrieved April 24, 2020, from https://www.mediapost.com/publications/article/326343/levis-credits-activism-with-surging-sales.html

[48] Bergh, C. (2014, July 14) The Dirty Jeans Manifesto. *linkedin.com.* retrieved April 24, 2020, from https://www.linkedin.com/pulse/20140714180558-14928043-the-dirty-jeans-manifesto/

[49] Kapner, S. & Chinni, D. (2019, November 19) Are Your Jeans Red or Blue? Shopping America's Partisan Divide. *wsj.com.* Retrieved April 24, 2020, from https://www.wsj.com/articles/are-your-jeans-red-or-blue-shopping-americas-partisan-divide-11574185777

Chapter 6

[1] http://www.myersbriggs.org/my-mbti-personality-type/my-mbti-results/how-frequent-is-my-type.htm

[2] Steinman, C. (2016, March 10) Hotwire's Campaign Targets Spontaneous Travelers. *mediapost.com.* Retrieved March 11, 2016, from http://www.mediapost.com/publications/article/270938/hotwires-campaign-targets-spontaneous-travelers.html?utm_source=newsletter&utm_medium=email&utm_content=headline&utm_campaign=91050

[3] Yale attitude change approach. *wikipedia.org.* Retrieved April 6, 2020, from https://en.wikipedia.org/wiki/Yale_attitude_change_approach#cite_ref-:8_28-0

[4] Haugtvedt, C., Petty, R., Cacioppo, J. (1992) Journal of Consumer Psychology. Retrieved May 11, 2016, from

http://www.researchgate.net/profile/John_Cacioppo/publication/223653300_Need_for_Cognition_and_Advertising_Understanding_the_Role_of_Personality_Variables_in_Consumer_Behavior/links/5432c00f0cf22395f29c492e.pdf

[5] (1998) Multicultural Use of the MBTI. *myersbriggs.org.* Retrieved March 19, 2020, from https://www.myersbriggs.org/more-about-personality-type/international-use/multicultural-use-of-the-mbti.htm

Chapter 7

[1] Tierney, J. (2011, August 17) Do You Suffer From Decision Fatigue? *nytimes.com.* Retrieved May 30, 2016, from http://www.nytimes.com/2011/08/21/magazine/do-you-suffer-from-decision-fatigue.html?_r=0

[2] Joutz, M. (2018, November 12) Get a Handle on Your Pots and Pans. *nytimes.com.* Retrieved May 1, 2020, from https://www.nytimes.com/2018/11/12/style/millennial-cookware-dutch-oven.html

[3] Howe, N. (2015, February 11) Millennials Don't Want To 'Embrace Failure' *forbes.com.* retrieved May 1, 2020, from https://www.forbes.com/sites/neilhowe/2015/02/11/millennials-dont-want-to-embrace-failure/#79ff4f43c19a

[4] Tierney, J. (2011, August 17) Do You Suffer From Decision Fatigue? *nytimes.com.* Retrieved March 21, 202, from http://www.nytimes.com/2011/08/21/magazine/do-you-suffer-from-decision-fatigue.html?_r=0

[5] Davidai, S., Gilovich, T. & Ross, L. (2012, July 30) The meaning of default options for potential organ donors. *Proceedings of the National Academy of Sciences.* Retrieved April 30, 2020, from https://stanford.app.box.com/s/yohfziywajw3nmwxo7d3ammndihibe7g

[6] (2019, August 30) The Psychology of Decision Making. *open.edu.* Retrieved March 21, 2020, from http://www.open.edu/openlearn/body-mind/psychology/the-psychology-decision-making

[7] Tang, C. (2020, March 27) 'Only 2 Left in Stock! Order Now!' But Does That Really Work? *wsj.com.* Retrieved May 1, 2020, from https://www.wsj.com/articles/only-2-left-in-stock-order-now-but-does-that-really-work-11585339621

[8] Zhao, G., Muehling, D., Singh, S., Chai, J. (2010) *Association For Consumer Research.* Retrieved May 31, 2016, from http://www.acrwebsite.org/volumes/v38/acr_v38_15920.pdf

[9] Imber, A. (2018, September 11) Why Eating the Same Thing for Breakfast Every Day Helps You Make Better Decisions. *entrepreneur.com.* Retrieved March 25, 2020, from https://www.entrepreneur.com/article/319838

[10] McLeod, S. (2016) What is Conformity? *simplypsychology.org.* Retrieved March 20, 2020, from https://www.simplypsychology.org/conformity.html

[11] Martin, C. (1997) Looking at Type: The Fundamentals *myersbriggs.org.* Retrieved March 20, 2020, from https://www.myersbriggs.org/my-mbti-personality-type/mbti-basics/thinking-or-feeling.htm

[12] Asch, S. (1951) Effects of Group Pressure Upon The Modification And Distortion Of Judgments. *Social Psychology.* Retrieved March 20, 2020, from https://www.gwern.net/docs/psychology/1952-asch.pdf

[13] Gopnik, A. (2014, September 12) Humans Naturally Follow Crowd Behavior. *wsj.com.* Retrieved May 31, 2016, from http://www.wsj.com/articles/humans-naturally-follow-crowd-behavior-1410543908

[14] Anik, L. & Norton, M. (2019, June 17) How Charities Can Use 'Tipping Points' To Get You to Donate. *wsj.com.* Retrieved April 30, 2020, from https://www.wsj.com/articles/how-charities-can-use-tipping-points-to-get-you-to-donate-11560736920

[15] Nagin, D. (2013, April 3) Deterrence: A Review of the Evidence by a Criminologist for Economists. *Annual Review of Economics.* retrieved April 30, 2020, from https://www.annualreviews.org/doi/pdf/10.1146/annurev-economics-072412-131310

[16] Bonavia, T. & Bronx-Ponce, J. (2018, February 14) Shame in decision making under risk conditions: Understanding the effect of transparency. *nih.gov.* Retrieved April 30, 2020, from https://www.ncbi.nlm.nih.gov/pmc/articles/PMC5812579/

[17] Fox, C., Linder, J. & Doctor, J. (2016, March 27) To Get Doctors to Do the Right Thing, Try Comparing Them to Their Peers. *wsj.com.* Retrieved April 27, 2020, from https://www.wsj.com/articles/to-get-doctors-to-do-the-right-thing-try-comparing-them-to-their-peers-1466993340

[18] https://en.wikiquote.org/wiki/H._L._Mencken

[19] Solnick, S. & Hemenway, D. (1997, April 2) Is more always better?: A survey on positional concerns. *Journal of Economic Behavior & Organization.* Vol 37 (1998) 373-383. Retrieved August 11, 2015, from http://isites.harvard.edu/fs/docs/icb.topic620591.files/Indices_of_Well being/HSPH.pdf

[20] Pinker, S. (2019, June 14) The Worst Form of Envy? In the Future Tense. *wsj.com.* Retrieved April 28, 2020, from https://www.wsj.com/articles/the-worst-form-of-envy-in-the-future-tense-11560527404

[21] The Rule of Obligation - How to Get Anyone to Do a Favor for You. *Westside Toastmasters.* Retrieved June 2, 2016, from http://westsidetoastmasters.com/resources/laws_persuasion/chap1.html

[22] Cialdini, R. (2001, October) Harnessing the Science of Persuasion. *Harvard Business Review.* Retrieved May 7, 2020, from https://dl1.cuni.cz/pluginfile.php/338220/mod_resource/content/2/Harnessing%20the%20Science%20of%20Persuasion.pdf

[23] Wollan, M. (2019, December 15) How to Keep a Stranger on the Line. *nytimes.com.* Retrieved May 18, 2020, from https://www.nytimes.com/2019/12/11/magazine/how-to-keep-a-stranger-on-the-phone.html

[24] Kitterman, T. (2020, February 18) Report: 83% of millennials want brands to align with tghem on values. *prdaily.com.* Retrieved March 27, 2020, from https://www.prdaily.com/report-83-of-millennials-want-brands-to-align-with-them-on-values/

[25] Baca, M. (2020, June 16) Roger Goodell: I 'encourage' a team to sign QB Colin Kaepernick. *nfl.com.* Retrieved July 11, 2020, from https://www.nfl.com/news/roger-goodell-i-encourage-a-team-to-sign-qb-colin-kaepernick

[26] Stillman, J. (2018, September 5) Here's the Data That Proves That Nike's Colin Kaepernick Ad Is Smart Marketing. *inc.com.* Retrieved March 18, 2020, from https://www.inc.com/jessica-stillman/heres-data-that-proves-nikes-colin-kaepernick-ad-is-seriously-smart-marketing.html

[27] Thomas, P. (2018, December 20) Nike Strides to Strong Sales Growth. *wsj.com.* Retrieved March 18, 2020, from https://www.wsj.com/articles/nike-strides-to-strong-sales-growth-11545344680

[28] Chin, K. (2019, December 20) Nike Sales Jump 10% Despite Split With Amazon. *wsj.com.* Retrieved March 18, 2020, from https://www.marketscreener.com/NIKE-INC-13739/news/Nike-Sales-Jump-10-Despite-Split-With-Amazon-WSJ-29754887/

[29] Murray, P. (2013, February 26) How Emotions Influence What We Buy. *Psychology Today.* Retrieved May 30, 2016, from https://www.psychologytoday.com/blog/inside-the-consumer-mind/201302/how-emotions-influence-what-we-buy

[30] Matchar, E. (2015, May 1) Sorry, Etsy. That Handmade Scarf Won't Save the World. *nytimes.com.* Retrieved May 20, 2020, from https://www.nytimes.com/2015/05/03/opinion/sunday/that-handmade-scarf-wont-save-the-world.html

[31] Clothier, M., Naughton, K., O'Leary, M., & Bloomberg News (2014, November 4) Lincoln Rides McConaughey Spoof to Best October in 7 Years. *chicagotribune.com.* Retrieved March 20, 2020, from https://www.chicagotribune.com/autos/sns-wp-blm-news-bc-lincoln-spoof04-20141104-story.html

[32] Houston, G. (2016, May 9) Millennials Are Really Into Red Lobster. *food and wine.com.* Retrieved May 11, 2016, from http://www.foodandwine.com/blogs/millennials-are-really-red-lobster

[33] Cameron, D., Inzlicht, M., and Cunningham, W. (2015, July 10) Empathy Is Actually a Choice. *nytimes.com.* Retrieved May 31, 2016, from http://www.nytimes.com/2015/07/12/opinion/sunday/empathy-is-actually-a-choice.html?_r=0

[34] Flaherty, C. (2017, January 13) Study of online ratings of professors suggest scores vary with instructor's gender and perceived rigor. https://www.insidehighered.com/news/2017/01/13/study-online-ratings-professors-suggest-scores-vary-instructors-gender-and-perceived
[35] Akst, D. (2016, August 26) Yes, Students Do Learn More From Attractive Teachers. *wsj.com.* Retrieved May 6, 2020, from https://www.wsj.com/articles/yes-students-do-learn-more-from-attractive-teachers-1472223974

[36] Morgado, P., Sousa, N., & Cerqueira, J.J. (2015) The Impact of Stress in Decision Making in the Context of Uncertainty. *Journal of Neuroscience Research.* Retrieved March 26, 2020, from https://repositorium.sdum.uminho.pt/bitstream/1822/51412/1/morgado%2C%20j%20neurosci%20res%2C%202015.pdf

[37] Maier, S., Makwana, A. & Hare, T. (2015, August 5) Acute Stress Impairs Self-Control in Goal-Directed Choice by Altering Multiple Functional Connections within the Brain's Decision Circuits. *Neuron* Retrieved June 5 2018 from https://www.cell.com/neuron/fulltext/S0896-6273(15)00627-3

Chapter 8

[1] Neff, J. (2007, September 24). Soft Soap. *Advertising Age.*

[2] Jeffers, M. (2005, September 12) Behind Dove's 'Real Beauty'. *Adweek.* p. 34-35.

Chapter 9

[1] Ricco, R.B. (2008) The Influence of argument structure on judgments of argument strength, function and adequacy. *The Quarterly Journal of Experimental Psychology,* 61 (4), 641-664

[1] Gilbert, D., Tafarodi, R. & Malone, P. (1993, August) You Can't Not Believe Everything You Read. *Journal of Personality and Social Psychology.* Retrieved April 3, 2020, from http://www.danielgilbert.com/Gilbert%20et%20al%20(EVERYTHING%20YOU%20READ).pdf

[2] Lowe, A. (2012) A Special Place in Our Minds: Examining the Serial Position Effect. *The Huron University College Journal of Learning and Motivation.* Retrieved May 30, 2016, from http://ir.lib.uwo.ca/cgi/viewcontent.cgi?article=1074&context=hucjlm

[3] Krugman, H. (1965, May 15) The Impact of Television Advertising: Learning Without Involvement. *semanticscholar.org* Retrieved April 6, 2020, from https://pdfs.semanticscholar.org/1ec9/28df48c1b96918304ec2bcc413d278cf6fdd.pdf

[4] Murre, J. and Dros, J. (2015, July 6) Replication and Analysis of Ebbinghaus' Forgetting Curve. *ncbi.nim.nih.gov.* Retrieved May 28, 2016, from http://www.ncbi.nlm.nih.gov/pmc/articles/PMC4492928/

[5] Herbert E. Krugman. (1972) Why Three Exposures May Be Enough. *Journal of Advertising Research* 12, 6 (1972): 11-14

[6] George A. Miller. (1956) The Magical Number Seven, Plus or Minus Two. *The Psychological Review*, vol. 63, Issue 2, pp. 81-97

[7] Tenenbaum, J. and Xy, F. (1999) Word learning as Bayesian inference. *mit.edu.* Retrieved May 29, 2016, from http://web.mit.edu/cocosci/Papers/cogsci00_FINAL.pdf

[8] Effective Frequency. *wikipedia.com.* Retrieved April 7, 2020, from https://en.wikipedia.org/wiki/Effective_frequency

[9] Butcher, S. (2019, February 4) Marketing & Business Development: How Many "Touches" Before a Sale? *jdbengineering.com.* Retrieved April 6, 2020, from https://jdbengineering.com/marketing-business-development-many-touches-sale/

[10] Krugman, H. (1965, May 15) The Impact Of Television Advertising: Learning Without Involvement. *semanticscholar.org.* Retrieved April 7, 2020, from https://pdfs.semanticscholar.org/1ec9/28df48c1b96918304ec2bcc413d278cf6fdd.pdf

[11] Bourke, C. (2014, November 24) Re-Defining Mobile Advertising Frequency. *digitalmarketingmagazine.co.uk* Retrieved April 7, 2020, from http://digitalmarketingmagazine.co.uk/digital-marketing-advertising/re-defining-mobile-advertising-frequency/1205

[12] (2012, February) Do TV Ads "Wear Out"? *Millward Brown.* Retrieved April 7, 2020, from https://www.rtrends.ru/netcat_files/File/MillwardBrown_KnowledgePoint_DoTvAdsWearout.pdf

[13] Fazio, L., Brashier, N., Payne, B. & Marsh, E. (2015, August 24) Knowledge Does Not Protect Against Illusory Truth. *Journal of Experimental Psychology.* Retrieved April 3, 2020, from https://www.apa.org/pubs/journals/features/xge-0000098.pdf

[14] McLeod, S. (2018, February 5) Cognitive Dissonance. *simplypsychology.org* Retrieved April 3, 2020, from, https://www.simplypsychology.org/cognitive-dissonance.html

Chapter 11

[1] Shu, S. and Carlson, K. (2014, January) When Three Charms but Four Alarms. *Journal of Marketing.* Retrieved May 29, 2016, from http://www.anderson.ucla.edu/faculty/suzanne.shu/Shu%20Carlson%20Three%20in%20Persuasion.pdf

[2] Lumsdaine, A. & Janis, I. (1953) Resistance to "Counterpropaganda" Produced by One-Sided and Two-sided "Propaganda" Presentations. *The Public Opinion Quarterly.* Retrieved April 10, 2020, from https://www.jstor.org/stable/2746134?seq=1

[3] Payne, J. & Nadel, L. (2004). Sleep, dreams and memory consolidation: The role of the stress hormone cortisol. *Learning & memory.* Retrieved June 18, 2009 from http://learnmem.cshlp.org/content/11/6/671.full

[4] Alterio, M. (2003). Using Storytelling to Enhance Student Learning. *Higher Education Academy.* Retrieved May 29, 2016, from https://www.heacademy.ac.uk/enhancement/starter-tools/learning-through-storytelling

[5] Facenda, V. (2007, October 29) Stories, Not Facts Engage Consumers. *Adweek.* p9

[6] Teague, L. (2015, November 7) Off Duty: Eating & Drinking: Clink Different. *The Wall Street Journal.* pD1
[7] Marcus, G. & Duke, A. (2019, August 31) The Problem With Believing What We Are Told. *wsj.com.* Retrieved April 3, 2020, from

https://www.wsj.com/articles/the-problem-with-believing-what-were-told-11567224060

[8] https://en.wikipedia.org/wiki/Coca-Cola_Zero_Sugar

[9] Ziobro, P. (2011, December 3) Dr Pepper Slims Down Five More of Its Sodas. *wsj.com.* Retrieved May 14, 2020, from https://www.wsj.com/articles/SB10001424052970204012004577074461489485438

[10] Miller, C. (2016, February 25) Is Blind Hiring the Best Hiring? *nytimes.com.* retrieved April 13, 2020, from http://www.nytimes.com/2016/02/28/magazine/is-blind-hiring-the-best-hiring.html?_r=0

[11] Loftus, E. F., & Palmer, J. C. (1974). Reconstruction of auto-mobile destruction: An example of the interaction between language and memory. *Journal of Verbal Learning and Verbal behavior*, 13, 585-589. Retrieved April 13, 2020, from https://www.simplypsychology.org/loftus-palmer.html

[12] Levin, I. & Gaeth, G. (1988, December 1) How Consumers Are Affected by the Framing of Attribute Information Before and After Consuming the Product. *Journal of Consumer Research.* Retrieved April 13, 2020, from https://academic.oup.com/jcr/article-abstract/15/3/374/1793963

[13] Lahart, J. (2020, June 3) America's Economy Is Healing Slowly. *wsj.com.* Retrieved June 5, 2020, from https://www.wsj.com/articles/americas-economy-is-healing-slowly-11591203786

[14] Mzezewa, T. (2019, November 23) How to Rebrand a Country. *nytimes.com.* Retrieved May 14, 2020, from https://www.nytimes.com/2019/11/23/travel/rebrandng-croatia-colombia.html

[15] Trent, S. (2020, May 24) Why We Refuse to Spend Much Money on Apps. *wsj.com.* Retrieved May 28, 2020, from https://www.wsj.com/articles/why-we-refuse-to-spend-much-money-on-apps-11590328800

[16] Summerville, A & Roese, N. (2008, May) Dare to Compare: Fact-Based versus Simulation-Based Comparison in Daily Life. *nih.gov.* Retrieved May 18, 2020, from https://www.ncbi.nlm.nih.gov/pmc/articles/PMC2597832/

[17] Ellet, J. (202, September 20) 3 Reasons Samsung's Latest Advertising Poking Apple Is So Smart. *forbes.com.* Retrieved May 31, 2020, from https://www.forbes.com/sites/johnellett/2012/09/20/3-reasons-samsungs-latest-advertising-poking-apple-is-so-smart/#38af32fa411e

[18] Standing, L. (1973) Learning 10,000 Pictures. *Quarterly Journal of Experimental Psychology.* Retrieved April 10, 2020, from https://www.researchgate.net/profile/Lionel_Standing/publication/232550420_Perception_and_memory_for_pictures_Single-trial_learning_of_2500_visual_stimuli/links/5911d05eaca27200fe39feba/Perception-and-memory-for-pictures-Single-trial-learning-of-2500-visual-stimuli.pdf

[19] Grady, C., McIntosh, A., Rajah, M., & Craik, F. (1998, March 3) Neural correlates of the episodic encoding of pictures and words. *pnas.org.* Retrieved April 10, 2020, from https://www.pnas.org/content/95/5/2703.full

[20] Joffe, H. (2008, February) The Power of Visual Material: Persuasion, Emotion and Identification. *Diogenes.* Retrieved April 10, 2020, from https://www.researchgate.net/publication/249742695_The_Power_of_Visual_Material_Persuasion_Emotion_and_Identification

[21] (2016, September 12) Text vs. Visuals – The Advantages of Each in Content Marketing *contentmarketing.com.* Retrieved April 10, 2020, from https://contentmarketing.com/2016/09/12/text-vs-visuals-the-advantages-of-each-in-content-marketing/

[22] Iyer, A. and Oldmeadow, J. (2006) 'Picture This: Emotional and Political Responses to Photographs of the Kenneth Bigley Kidnapping'. *European Journal of Social Psychology.* Retrieved April 10, 2020, from https://onlinelibrary.wiley.com/doi/abs/10.1002/ejsp.316

[23]https://en.wikipedia.org/wiki/Sandy_Hook_Elementary_School_shooting

[24] Webber, P. (2019, November 29) 5 Ways Graphics Can Boost Content Marketing Success. *mediapost.com.* Retrieved May 18, 2020, from

https://www.mediapost.com/publications/article/340127/5-ways-graphics-can-boost-content-marketing-succes.html

[25] Gnambs, T., Appel, M. & Oeberst, A. (2015, July 24) Red Color and Risk-Taking Behavior in Online Environments. *nih.gov* Retrieved April 23, 2020, from https://www.ncbi.nlm.nih.gov/pmc/articles/PMC4514790/

[26] Dockrill, P. (2016, March 23) Just Looking at Photos of Nature Could Be Enough to Lower Your Work Stress Levels. *sciencealert.com* Retrieved May 1, 2020, from https://www.sciencealert.com/just-looking-at-photos-of-nature-could-be-enough-to-lower-your-work-stress-levels

[27] Glezer, L., Kim, J., Rule, J., Jiang, X. & Riesenhuber, M. (2015, March 25) Adding Words to the Brain's Visual Dictionary: Novel Word Learning Selectively Sharpens Orthographic Representations in the VWFA. *The Journal of Neuroscience.* Retrieved April 13, 2020, from https://www.ncbi.nlm.nih.gov/pmc/articles/PMC4389595/

[28] Greenberg, K. (2015, October 9) Memorable Logos Drive Brand Affinity *mediapost.com.* Retrieved May 18, 2020, from https://www.mediapost.com/publications/article/260104/memorable-logos-drive-brand-affinity.html

[29] Arditi, A. & Cho, J. (2015, October 20) Serifs and font legibility. *Vision Research.* Retrieved April 22, 2020, from https://www.ncbi.nlm.nih.gov/pmc/articles/PMC4612630/

[30] Johnson, R., Bui, B., & Schmitt, L. (2018, April 24) Are two spaces better than one? The effect of spacing following periods and commas during reading. *Attention, Perception, & Psychophysics.* Retrieved April 22, 2020, from https://link.springer.com/article/10.3758/s13414-018-1527-6

[31] Schroll, R., Schnurr, B. & Grewal, D. (2018, March 10) Humanizing Products with Handwritten Typefaces. *Journal of Consumer Research.* Retrieved April 14, 2020, from https://academic.oup.com/jcr/article/45/3/648/4925803#120648450

[32] Rhodes, M. (2020, February 24) Startups Wrap Brand Identity With Sustainable Packaging. *wsj.com.* Retrieved April 14, 2020, from https://www.wsj.com/articles/startups-wrap-brand-identity-with-sustainable-packaging-11582466400

[33] Zmuda, N. (2009, April 2) Tropicana Line's Sales Plunge 20% Post-Rebranding. *adage.com.* Retrieved April 2 2009, from http://adage.com/article/news/tropicana-line-s-sales-plunge-20-post-rebranding/135735/

[34] Esterl, M. (2014, September 25) 'Share a Coke' Credited With a Pop in Sales. *wsj.com.* retrieved April 14, 2020, from https://www.wsj.com/articles/share-a-coke-credited-with-a-pop-in-sales-1411661519

[35] Dosh, K. (2019, August 8) Coca-Cola Unveils New NFL And College Football Packaging. *forbes.com.* Retrieved April 14, 2020, from https://www.forbes.com/sites/kristidosh/2019/08/08/coca-cola-unveils-new-nfl-and-college-football-packaging/#1a09d1973e78

[36] Menon, V. & Berger, J. (2007, August 1) Music moves brain to pay attention, Stanford study finds. *med.stanford.edu.* Retrieved April 2, 2020, from https://med.stanford.edu/news/all-news/2007/07/music-moves-brain-to-pay-attention-stanford-study-finds.html

[37] Dean, J. (2013, December 11) Music and memory: 5 Awesome New Psychology Studies. *PSYBLOG.* Retrieved April 2, 20202, from https://www.spring.org.uk/2013/12/music-and-memory-5-awesome-new-psychology-studies.php

[38] https://www.billboard.com/music/john-mellencamp/chart-history/country-airplay/song/512856

Chapter 12

[1] Chaker, A. (2016, September 14) September Is the Real New Year. *wsj.com.* Retrieved June 6, 2020, from https://www.wsj.com/articles/september-is-the-real-new-year-1473875636

[2] (2008, June 6). Gillette Fusion case study: developing a US$1 billion brand. *market-research-report.com.* Retrieved April 20, 2009 , from http://www.market-research-report.com/datamonitor/CSCM0171.htm

Chapter 14

[1] (2008, June 24). Understanding the True Value of Multi-platform Advertising. *IMMI; Integrated Media Measurement Inc.* Retrieved April 12, 2009, from http://www.immi.com/pdfs/2008-06-24_WP_Crossplatform.pdf

[2] Neff, J. (2010, July 26) How Much Old Spice Body Wash Has the Old Spice Guy Sold? *adage.com.* Retrieved June 3, 2020, from https://adage.com/article/news/spice-body-wash-spice-guy-sold/145096

[3] Aboulhosn, S. (2020, May 4) 18 Facebook statistics every marketer should know in 2020. *sproutsocial.com.* Retrieved May 21, 2020, from https://sproutsocial.com/insights/facebook-stats-for-marketers/

[4] Rijn, J. (2015) DMA National Client Email Report 2015. *emailmonday.com.* Retrieved May 26, 2020, from https://www.emailmonday.com/dma-national-client-email-report-2015/

[5] Aufreiter, N., Boudet, J. & Weng, V. (2014, January 1) Why marketers should keep sending you e-mails. *mckinsey.com.* Retrieved May 26, 2020, from https://www.mckinsey.com/business-functions/marketing-and-sales/our-insights/why-marketers-should-keep-sending-you-emails

[6] (2015) The New Rules of Email Marketing. *campaignmonitor.com.* Retrieved May 25, 2020, from https://www.campaignmonitor.com/resources/guides/email-marketing-new-rules/

[7] (2019) Email Trends Report: Mobile vs. Desktop. *campaignmonitor.com.* Retrieved May 25, 2020, from https://www.campaignmonitor.com/resources/guides/email-marketing-trends/

[8] (2019, February 28) The Surprising Data about How Often to Send Promotional Emails. *campaignmonitor.com.* Retrieved May 25, 2020, from https://www.campaignmonitor.com/blog/email-marketing/2019/02/the-surprising-data-about-how-often-to-send-promotional-emails/

[9] Wiseman, A. (2019, June 27) Email Marketing Frequency Best Practices in 2020. *smartmail.com.* Retrieved May 25, 2020, from https://www.smartrmail.com/blog/email-marketing-frequency-best-practices-2019/

[10] Maese, R. (2018, May 31) NBA Twitter: A sports bar that doesn't close, where the stars pull up a seat next to you. *washingtonpost.com.* Retrieved May 25, 2020 from https://www.washingtonpost.com/news/sports/wp/2018/05/31/nba-twitter-a-sports-bar-that-doesnt-close-where-the-stars-pull-up-a-seat-next-to-you/

[11] Noyes, D. (2020, May) The Top 20 Valuable Facebook Statistics – Updated May 2020. *zephoria.com.* Retrieved May 25, 2020, from https://zephoria.com/top-15-valuable-facebook-statistics/

[12] Patel, S. (2016, October 7) Apples and Oranges: Why a TV viewer does not equal an online viewer. *digiday.com.* Retrieved May 22, 2020, from https://digiday.com/media/apple-and-oranges/

[13] Volz, D. (2018, December 17) Russians Took Aim at Black Voters to Boost Trump, reports to Senate Find. *wsj.com* Retrieved December 19, 2018, from https://www.wsj.com/articles/russians-took-aim-at-black-voters-to-boost-trump-reports-to-senate-find-11545066563

[14] Worthy, P. (2018, September 26) Top Instagram Demographics That Matter to Social Media Marketers. *hootsuite.com.* Retrieved December 19, 2018, from https://blog.hootsuite.com/instagram-demographics/

[15] Terlep, S. & Seetharaman, D. (2016, August 17) *P&G to Scale Back Targeted Facebook Ads. wsj.com.* Retrieved May 25, 2020, from https://www.wsj.com/articles/p-g-to-scale-back-targeted-facebook-ads-1470760949

[16] Gallant, D. (2018, July 8) How to Beat the Zuckerberg Casino. *wsj.com.* Retrieved May 25, 2020, from https://www.wsj.com/articles/how-to-beat-the-zuckerberg-casino-1531075000

[17] Kornelis, C. (2019, April 26) Today, Anybody Can Be a Filmmaker. Here's What It Might Cost. *wsj.com.* Retrieved May 25, 2020, from https://www.wsj.com/articles/today-anybody-can-be-a-filmmaker-heres-what-it-might-cost-11556295944

[18] Taylor, E. (2013, January 23) Why Likes Don't Matter. *socialsamosa.com* Retrieved May 25, 2020, from http://www.socialsamosa.com/2013/01/why-likes-dont-matter/

[19] Seetharaman, D. (2015, October 14) What Celebrities Can Teach Companies About Social Media. *wsj.com.* Retrieved May 28, 2020, from https://www.wsj.com/articles/what-celebrities-can-teach-companies-about-social-media-1444788220

[20] McGee, M. (2011, April 14) Search Sends More & Better Traffic To Content Sites Than Social Media, Study Says. *searchengineland.com.* retrieved may 28, 2020, from https://searchengineland.com/search-sends-more-better-traffic-to-content-sites-than-social-media-study-says-72988

[21] Garcia, K. (2018, September 7) More Product Searches Start on Amazon. *emarketer.com.* Retrieved May 28, 2020, from https://www.emarketer.com/content/more-product-searches-start-on-amazon

[22] Smith, B. (2018, January 19) 15 Visual Content Marketing Statistics That'll Blow Your Mind. *jeffbullas.com.* Retrieved May 28, 2020, from https://www.jeffbullas.com/visual-content-marketing-statistics/

[23] *thinkwithgoogle.com.* Retrieved May 28, 2020, from https://www.thinkwithgoogle.com/data/shopping-video-research-statistics/

[24] (2016) 5 Stats That Prove Ecommerce Stores Need Video. *wyzowl.com.* Retrieved May 28, 2020, from https://www.wyzowl.com/5-stats-ecommerce-needs-video/

[25] Rudolph, S. (2015, July 25) The Impact of Online Reviews on Customers' Buying Decisions. *business2community.com.* Retrieved May 28, 2020, from https://www.business2community.com/infographics/impact-online-reviews-customers-buying-decisions-infographic-01280945

[26] Dolan, R. (2019, September 27) Have Online Reviews Lost All Value? *wsj.com.* Retrieved May 28, 2020, from https://www.wsj.com/articles/have-online-reviews-lost-all-value-11569606584

[27] Wootten, N. (2019, May 13) Why OOH Is Effective In Reaching Millennials And Gen Z. *mediapost.com.* Retrieved May 28, 2020, from https://www.mediapost.com/publications/article/335771/why-ooh-is-effective-in-reaching-millennials-and-g.html?edition=113859

[28] (2006, September). Interactive Billboards Land at Chicago. *Other Advertising*, p13

[29] (2015) Event & Experiential Marketing Industry. Forecast and Best Practices Study. *eventmarketer.com.* Retrieved may 28, 2020, from http://cdn.eventmarketer.com/wp-content/uploads/2016/01/EventTrack2015_Executive.pdf?_ga=1.2089073.1166920123.1464299493

[30] Troianovski, A. (2013, May 21) Phone Firms Sell Data on Customers. *wsj.com.* Retrieved May 28, 2020, from https://www.wsj.com/articles/SB10001424127887323463704578497153556847658

[31] Sallomi, P. (2018, December 11) Radio: Revenue, reach and resiliance. *deloitte.com.* Retrieved July 11, 2020, from https://www2.deloitte.com/us/en/insights/industry/technology/technology-media-and-telecom-predictions/radio-revenue.html

[32] https://news.iheart.com/featured/maria-milito/

[33]https://twitter.com/mariamilito?ref_src=twsrc%5Egoogle%7Ctwcamp%5Eserp%7Ctwgr%5Eauthor

[34] Winn, R. (2020, April 21) 2020 Podcast Stats & Facts. *podcastinsights.com.* Retrieved May 28, 2020, from https://www.podcastinsights.com/podcast-statistics/

[35] https://rainnews.com/infinite-dial-2020-smart-speaker-ownership-still-rising-with-radio-split-by-age/

[36] Martin, C. (2019, March 11) Consumers Tap Smart Speakers For Questions About Music. *mediapost.com* Retrieved March 13, 2019, from https://www.mediapost.com/publications/article/333048/consumers-tap-smart-speakers-for-questions-about-m.html?utm_source=newsletter&utm_medium=email&utm_content=headline&utm_campaign=113143&hashid=ybq2buULrntyGS6NfbELk0afrrI
[37] Faw, L. (2018, August 8) How Brands Can Avoid The Dreaded Voice Assistant 'Dismissal' *mediapost.com* Retrieved August 29, 2018, from https://www.mediapost.com/publications/article/323358/how-brands-can-avoid-the-dreaded-voice-assistant.html?utm_source=newsletter&utm_medium=email&utm_conte

nt=headline&utm_campaign=110385&hashid=ybq2buULrntyGS6NfbELk0afrrI

[38] Ives, N. (2019, June 17) The Ad Industry Has High Hopes for Direct-to-Consumer Businesses. *wsj.com.* retrieved May 21, 2020, from https://www.wsj.com/articles/the-ad-industry-has-high-hopes-for-direct-to-consumer-businesses-11560823381

[39] (2017, November 21) Why TV Remains the world's most effective advertising. *thinkbox.tv.* Retrieved May 22, from, https://www.thinkbox.tv/news-and-opinion/newsroom/why-tv-remains-the-worlds-most-effective-advertising/

[40] Ives, N. (2019, June 17) The Ad Industry Has High Hopes for Direct-to-Consumer Businesses. *wsj.com.* retrieved May 21, 2020, from https://www.wsj.com/articles/the-ad-industry-has-high-hopes-for-direct-to-consumer-businesses-11560823381

[41] Lafayette, J. (2018, March 29) Despite Cord-Cutting, Time -Shifting, TV Ads Still Yield Best ROI: Report. *multichannel.com.* Retrieved May 21, 2020, from https://www.multichannel.com/news/despite-cord-cutting-time-shifting-tv-ads-still-yield-best-roi-report-413180

[42] Vizard, S. (2019, November 21) TV the 'least risky' form of advertising, finds new research. *marketingweek.com.* Retrieved May 21, 2020, from https://www.marketingweek.com/tv-least-risky-form-of-advertising/

[43] Patel, S. (2016, October 7) Apples and Oranges: Why a TV viewer does not equal an online viewer. *digiday.com.* Retrieved May 22, 2020, from https://digiday.com/media/apple-and-oranges/

[44] (2019, March 4) Understanding Campaign Audiences Across TV + Digital. *nielsen.com.* Retrieved May 22, 2020, from https://www.nielsen.com/us/en/insights/article/2019/understanding-campaign-audiences-across-tv-and-digital/

[45] (2016, June 17) Why ROI Data Is The Future Of TV Advertising. *simulmedia.com.* Retrieved May 22, from, https://www.simulmedia.com/news/2016/06/17/why-roi-data-is-the-future-of-tv-advertising/

[46] (2017, November 21) Why TV Remains the world's most effective advertising. *thinkbox.tv.* Retrieved May 22, from, https://www.thinkbox.tv/news-and-opinion/newsroom/why-tv-remains-the-worlds-most-effective-advertising/

[47] Wilmarth, A. (2019, January 17) Is Television Still King? *bankingjournal.aba.com.* Retrieved May 22, from, https://bankingjournal.aba.com/2019/01/is-television-still-king/

[48] (2018, December 11) How the Median Age of TV Viewers Differs Across Platforms. *marketingcharts.com.* retrieved May 22, 2020, from https://www.marketingcharts.com/television/tv-audiences-and-consumption-106649

[49] (2019, June 19) Table 11A. Time spent in leisure and sports activities for the civilian population by selected characteristics, averages per day, 2018 annual averages. *census.gov.* Retrieved May 22, 2020, from https://www.bls.gov/news.release/atus.t11A.htm

[50] Perlberg, S. (2014, November 20) Targeted Ads Are Coming to Your Television. *wsj.com.* Retrieved May 22, 2020, from https://www.wsj.com/articles/targeted-ads-tv-can-do-that-now-too-1416506504

[51] Rosman, K. (2013, August 14) Weather Channel Now Also Forecasts What You'll Buy. *wsj.com.* Retrieved May 22, 2020, from https://www.wsj.com/articles/weather-channel-now-also-forecasts-whats-youll-buy-1376522336

[52] Rutenberg, J. (2013, June 20) Data You Can Believe In. *nytimes.com.* Retrieved may 25, 2020, from https://www.nytimes.com/2013/06/23/magazine/the-obama-campaigns-digital-masterminds-cash-in.html

[53] Watson, A. (2019, August 13) Number of magazine readers in the United States from 2012 to 2018*(in millions) statista.com.* Retrieved May 25, 2020, from https://www.statista.com/statistics/207850/total-gross-magazine-audience-in-the-united-states/

[54] Watson, A. (2019, August 27) U.S. Magazine Industry - Statistics & Facts. *statista.com.* Retrieved May 25, 2020, from https://www.statista.com/topics/1265/magazines/

[55] (2020) Magazine Publishing Trends For 2020 - The Alliance Of Print And Digital. *ovidbell.com.* retrieved May 25, 2020, from https://www.ovidbell.com/magazine-publishing-trends-for-2020-the-alliance-of-print-and-digital/

[56] Braverman, B. (2019, January 8) How to Future-Proof Your Print Magazines. *foliomag.com.* Retrieved May 25, 2020, from https://www.foliomag.com/future-proof-print-magazines/

[57] (2018, June 19) Digital Magazine Audience Grows, Still Lags Print. *marketingcharts.com.* Retrieved May 25, 2020, from https://www.marketingcharts.com/cross-media-and-traditional/magazines-traditional-and-cross-channel-83731

[58] Oloizia, J. (2014, August 21) The Facts and Figures Behind Vogue Magazine. *nytimes.com.* Retrieved May 25, 2020, from https://www.nytimes.com/2014/08/21/t-magazine/vogue-magazine-facts-and-figures-chart.html

[59] Buss, D. 92013, April 12) Conde Nast Extends Magazine Brands into Bar and Restaurant Scene. *brandchannel.com.* retrieved May 25, 2020 from https://www.brandchannel.com/2013/04/12/conde-nast-extends-magazine-brands-into-bar-and-restaurant-scene/

[60] Trachtenberg, J. (2019, May 28) Sports Illustrated Sold for $110 Million to Licensing Company Authentic Brands. *wsj.com.* Retrieved May 15, 2020, from https://www.wsj.com/articles/sports-illustrated-sold-for-110-million-to-licensing-company-authentic-brands-11559005320

[61] Grieco, E. (2020, February 14) Fast facts about the newspaper industry's financial struggles as McClatchy files for bankruptcy. *pewresearch.org.* retrieved May 25, 2020, from https://www.pewresearch.org/fact-tank/2020/02/14/fast-facts-about-the-newspaper-industrys-financial-struggles/

[62] 2018) WSJ. The World's Leading Luxury Magazine. *dowjones.com.* Retrieved May 25, 2020, from https://images.dowjones.com/wp-content/uploads/sites/183/2018/05/09164157/WSJ.-Magazine-2018-Media-Kit-1.pdf

Chapter 15

[1] Hernandez, G. & Johnson, G. (2000, July 19) Taco Bell Replaces Chief. Chihuahua as Sales Fall. *latimes.com.* Retrieved May 30, 2020, from

https://www.latimes.com/archives/la-xpm-2000-jul-19-fi-55188-story.html

[2] Bednarski, P. (2019, September 17) P&G's Secret Brand Will Buy 9,000 Tickets to Women's Pro Soccer Games. *mediapost.com.* Retrieved September 18, 2019, from https://www.mediapost.com/publications/article/340772/pgs-secret-brand-will-buy-9000-tickets-to-women.html

[3] Al-Muslim, A. (2018, June 17) The Making of the Tide Ad That Scored in the Super Bowl. *wsj.com.* Retrieved May 30, 2020, from https://www.wsj.com/articles/the-making-of-the-tide-ad-that-scored-in-the-super-bowl-1529285099

Index

R

S

T

CPSIA information can be obtained
at www.ICGtesting.com
Printed in the USA
LVHW051721030621
689279LV00009B/1005